SPACE, SCIENCE AND OTHER THINGS -

ELEMENTARY (K-8) INTERACTIVE

SANDRA BOJTOS HART

Other books by Sandra Hart:

<u>Somewhere Out There</u> – Time Travel Romance
Written under the name of Sandra Cam Hart
ISBN 1-4116-5784-5

<u>Space Show</u> – Colored copy of <u>Space, Science and Other Things –
Elementary (K-8) Interactive Space Show</u>
ISBN 1-4116-4731-9

Published by Hartflame Productions

Cover design by Sandra Hart

ISBN 1-4116-4674-6

Dedication

To my husband, Colonel Michael Charles Hart, USAF,
whose encouragement and help brought this book
from an idea to a reality, and to my many students,
whose love for "Science and Space" made my job
easy and most of all fun!

And to

The staff and instructors of
International Space Camp - 1996
Space Camp, Huntsville, Alabama.
Participating in the program changed my life forever
and gave me a new quest for knowledge.
Thank you for the experience of a lifetime!

Wishing you all the best!
May your teaching endeavors soar
you to the stars and may your
students enjoy their journey to
success!

Sandra Bojtos-Hart
'96

Sandra Bojtos Hart is the 1996 National State Teacher of the
Year - Territory of Guam and the
1999 Department of Defense Teacher of the Year -
Guam District

To the Teacher

This resource manual is intended to make teaching "Science and Space Science" more meaningful to your students. As one of the 1996 National State Teachers of the Year, I had the opportunity to attend a ten-day, International Space Camp held in Huntsville, Alabama. Teachers of the year from all 50 states, the District of Columbia, Guam, Puerto Rico, and the Commonwealth of the Northern Mariana Islands, attended the camp sponsored by a $70,000 grant from NASA. The Space and Rocket Center paid for the International students and Coca Cola picked up the tab for the International teachers with a $50,000 grant.

The space campers and teachers studied space shuttle operations, crew systems, rocketry, toured the Marshall Space Flight Center and were able to speak to astronauts aboard the shuttle. The teachers also got the chance to fly in single-engine airplanes. Leading scientists from the U.S. were flown into Space Camp to teach classes in hydroponics and satellite topography. Members of Werner Von Braun's rocket team were also on hand to teach classes in rocketry.

Needless to say, the experience changed my life forever. Upon returning to my classroom, I researched ways to include what I had just learned into my everyday lessons to help my students foster a love of science and especially space science. The result of my time and effort produced a school-wide, interactive "Chemistry and Physics Show" using a space theme with my students being the actors, complete with aliens and a mock nose cone of the space shuttle, Endeavor.

The show included science, space science, magic, music, and most of all a ton of fun. The highly interactive presentation used approximately 55 students from the audience in the course of an hour and a half. Students from the audience were brought up on stage to do the experiments, reinforcing my philosophy of education…**"Tell me and I forget. Show me and I remember. Involve me and I understand."**

Over the years I have presented the show with my first, second and fifth grade students. I have also done the show at other schools without my classroom students and only used audience participation. The audience has been as large as five hundred students and parents, to as little as forty students.

Since becoming Teacher of the Year I have offered many workshops to other teachers on using science in their classroom to teach reading and math. I have taught other teachers how to build the cabin of the space shuttle and have been rewarded with the fact that teachers are actually using my lessons to enhance their lessons.

This resource manual was written with the hopes of passing on my extreme love of science to you in a fun and exhilarating way. It is such a reward to see students excited about science and to see them screaming and yelling for more. This show will hopefully make science more appealing and fresh to young minds. I will walk you through the entire show and pass on my tips to you. Use as much of the book as you need for your production and most of all; add your own spark of creation to the performance. Please bear in mind that I'm not a professional writer, nor do I claim to be, but an ordinary classroom teacher who tried to put my show into details for other teachers. My style of writing is more of a personal style talking to teachers and walking them through the production in every aspect of the show.

May the force be with you and see you in space.

Warmest Regards,
Sandra Bojtos Hart

Bojsan@aol.com

For Privacy reasons, student faces have been blocked out

Descriptive Table of Contents

(Author's comments) Explains the rationale and philosophy behind the manual.

(Outline of the show) This is the sheet(s) that the teacher will use on stage during the production; a reminder of what comes next, a cheat sheet or script to follow for the experiments and activities. The teacher will be able to refer to the manifest during the entire production.

(Step-by-step instructions for the entire production) directs the teacher through the entire show. This chapter will have all of the script and dialogue for the teacher and students. (Integrates – art, math, language arts, science, music)

(Sample program for the show) shows an example of a program that teachers can make for the audience. The program is great for parents/teachers to take home for them to use as a reminder of the experiments in the production so they can try some of them at home/school. The program will give credit to the students in the production or any other helper/volunteers.

(Where to buy materials and how to use the tricks) explains the magic tricks used in the opening of the show in a little more detail and lists the web sites and prices for purchasing the materials used in the production. Teachers do not have to use the magic tricks or spend extra money for the production, but this chapter is included for the teachers who want to be a bit more creative in the show. Every student loves magic as it is great attention grabber and builds excitement for the production.

17 Vocabulary Words

(Words taken from the production) lists new vocabulary words used during the production to reinforce the teaching in the production. The chapter also gives some simple activities to do with the vocabulary words. (Integrates - language arts, science)

18 Curriculum Standards & Objectives

(K-6 Science Objectives) objectives taken from the Department of Defense Dependent Schools web site and used to create objectives for the space show. The objectives can be adapted and used to fit other school districts' curriculum standards and objectives. The objectives are used as models for creating new objectives for science.

19 Follow-up

(Student products) shows the different ways students can share their experiences of attending the show (drawing, writing, computer-aided drawing/writing). This will give teachers examples of the various mediums the students can use to write creatively. (Integrates - language arts, art, computers, science)

20 Acknowledgements

(Credits) acknowledges the web sites and people who contributed to the making of the manual.

21 Appendix

(Full-size copies)

Section A - full-size copy of the program.

Section B - names for the back of the Space Camp T-Shirts - copy them, cut them out, and tape them to the back of the shirts.

Section C - full-size certificates - copy on a copier and use for production or use them for ideas for making new certificates.

Section D - extended directions for a full spacecraft (orbiter cabin, cargo bay, thrusters) - with permission from the Education Department of U.S. Space Camp, Huntsville, AL.

Chapter 1

Show Manifest

During the show you will need an accessible outline of the presentation to guide or remind you of each experiment. Put the manifest into a clear, plastic, page protector to prevent any liquid from spilling on it and destroying it during the presentation. Attach it to a clipboard for easy access and have it handy on the side of your table while on stage. It will be easy to access, reminding you of each experiment in the show.

There are two show manifests in this chapter. Use **Manifest #1** if you are using your classroom students. Use **Manifest #2** if you are presenting the show by yourself without the aid of your students.

Manifest #1

- List student names on the manifest where they will be needed in the show. There are parts in the show where the students come up to the microphone and read a scientific fact. If you don't want your students to read between the experiments, you can choose a section in the show when they all come up to the microphone and read their student quotes one right after the other.

- Student readings (Students will read a scientific quote to the audience.) Divide the students into groups of three (e.g., Group A, Group B, and Group C). **See Chapter 8 - Student Scientific Quotes, page 122.**

- While your students are reading their scientific quotes, have other classroom students go out into the audience to pick volunteers for an experiment. **See Manifest #1 for an example.**

Example, Say:
"Tom, Ken and Mary Ann (Group A), come up to the microphone. Randy and Pamala, get two people from the audience."

This gives your students sitting on stage a chance to participate in the show other then during their readings.

- The number of students you have in your classroom will determine how many times you can send your students out into the audience to pick volunteers. If you have a large class, you will only use that student one time to pick an audience volunteer. Alternately, if you have a small class, you can have each student go out into the audience numerous times to get volunteers from the audience.

- The manifest should also indicate the number of volunteers you will need for each experiment (e.g., **Sound Vibrations...Chicken Cups – <u>12 people from the audience</u>**). Listing the number of people or volunteers needed for the experiments will help you remember how many volunteers will be needed at that time in the show.
- Be creative and make your own format for the readings and put the students into the show where you feel it would be best.

Manifest #2

- Use Manifest #2 if you are doing the show without the help of your students.

Manifest # 1 – Introduction - rules for presentation

* **Endeavor Landing Play**

* **Science is Magic - Magic tricks** - Floating ball, Lota Bowl, Red Hanky, Disappearing mouse, Color Changing Hanky, Card & Orange Trick (any other trick you want to do)

* **I'VE GOT THE POWER – MUSIC** - D'lite thumbs - **4 people from the audience** (Student #1 and Student # 2 - Each of you get two people from the audience.)

* **Knowledge is Power** - Ping-pong Balls - **4 smart people from the audience** - **Open/Closed Circuits** (Student #3 and Student # 4 - Each of you get two people from the audience.)

* **Chemical/Physical Changes** - Magic Paper

* **Mission: Knowledge is Power** - Yell it to the audience.
* **ALIENS!** Run across stage and hide. ****************************

Student Name, Student Name, Student Name - Come up to the microphone - Group A

* **Matter** - balloons

* **Balloon Pop with pin** - **1 person from the audience** (Student #5 - Get one person from the audience.)

* **Acids/Bases - vinegar and baking soda** - experiments

* **Mission: Knowledge is Power** - Yell it to the audience.
* **ALIENS!** Run across stage and hide. ****************************

Student Name, Student Name, Student Name - Come up to the microphone - Group B

* **Air Bags** - **12 people from the audience** (Student #6, #7, #8, #9 #10, #11 - Each of you get two people from the audience.)

Student Name, Student Name, Student Name - Come up to the microphone - Group C

* **Sound Vibrations** - Chicken Cups - **12 people from the audience** (Student #12, #13, #14, #15, #16, #17 - Each of you get two people from the audience.)

<u>Student Name, Student Name, Student Name - Come up to the microphone - Group D</u>

* **Shuttle Telephone** - Sound vibrations - <u>**2 people from the audience**</u> (Student #18 - Get two people from the audience.)

* **Mission: Knowledge is Power** - Yell it to the audience.
* **ALIENS!** Run across stage/drop signs and then come out and catch the teacher. *************************************

* **Forces** - Centrifugal Force - bucket of water

<u>Student Name, Student Name, Student Name - Come up to the microphone - Group E</u>

* **Bottle Fountain** - <u>**1 person from the audience**</u>
  (Student #19 - Get one person from the audience.)

* **Rocket Launcher** - <u>**2 people from the audience**</u> (Student #20 and Student #21 - Each of you get one person from the audience.)

<u>Student Name, Student Name, Student Name - Come up to the microphone - Group F</u>

* **Balloon Race** - Opposite and Equal Reaction - <u>**2 people from the audience**</u> (Student #22 and Student # 23 - Each of you get one person from the audience.)

<u>Student Name, Student Name, Student Name - Come up to the microphone - Group G</u>

* **Forces**...Crushing Egg in hand - <u>**12 people from the audience**</u> (Student #, #, #, #, #, # - Each of you get two people from the audience.)

* **Hoberman Sphere** - expanding/contracting - <u>**3 people from the audience**</u> (Student #, #, #, - Each of you get one person from the audience.)

* **Crushing Cans** - with air pressure

* **Alcohol/Water** - experiment

* **Van de Graaf Generator** - static electricity, hair raising - Use yourself or volunteers from the audience
* **Mission Control Song** - Salute the audience and bow together

Manifest # 2 – Introduction – rules for presentation

* **Science is Magic – Magic tricks** – Floating ball, Lota Bowl, Red Hanky, Disappearing mouse, Color Changing Hanky, Card & Orange Trick (any other trick you want to do)

* **I'VE GOT THE POWER – MUSIC** – D'lite thumbs – **4 people from the audience**

* **Knowledge is Power** – Ping-pong Balls – **4 smart people from the audience** – **Open/Closed Circuits**

* **Chemical/Physical Changes** – Magic Paper

* **Mission: Knowledge is Power** – Yell it to the audience.
* **ALIENS!** Run across stage and hide. ****************************

* **Matter** – balloons

* **Balloon Pop with pin** – **1 person from the audience**

* **Acids/Bases – vinegar and baking soda** – experiments

* **Mission: Knowledge is Power** – Yell it to the audience.
* **ALIENS!** Run across stage and hide. ****************************

* **Air Bags** – **12 people from the audience**

* **Sound Vibrations** – Chicken Cups – **12 people from the audience**

* **Shuttle Telephone** – Sound vibrations – **2 people from the audience**

* **Mission: Knowledge is Power** – Yell it to the audience.
* **ALIENS!** Run across stage/drop signs and then come out and catch the teacher. **

* **Forces** – Centrifugal Force – bucket of water

* **Bottle Fountain** – **1 person from the audience**

* **Rocket Launcher** – **2 people from the audience**

* **Balloon Race** – Opposite and Equal Reaction – **2 people from the audience**

* **Forces** - Crushing Egg in hand - <u>**12 people from the audience**</u>

* **Hoberman Sphere** - expanding/contracting - <u>**3 people from the audience**</u>

* **Crushing Cans** - with air pressure

* **Alcohol/Water** - experiment

* **Van de Graaf Generator** - static electricity, hair rising

Chapter 2

Teacher's Guide

This chapter will guide you through the entire production giving step-by-step instructions for each operation from beginning to end. ***Note** - Please see the other chapters for more detailed information on specific topics.

Be innovative and add your own spark of imagination to the production to make it your own or use the resources in this manual to reproduce my creation. Either way, you and your students will embark on a wonderful journey of space, science and other things.

If you are not doing the production with your classroom students, please skip over the instructions for student parts.

Stage Set Up

Stage set up will take about 1 ½ hours if you do all of the work yourself, so allow time accordingly. The best place to hold the production is in a theater where you are elevated above the audience with ample room on either side of the stage for the aliens to hide. If you present the production in one large room like the cafeteria or gym, you will need to make two folding screens out of some large cardboard boxes or use devices to hide the aliens from the audience. Place a screen on both sides of the stage so the aliens can run from one screen to the other. **See Chapter 10 - Aliens, page 134.**

Space Shuttle Orbiter – should be positioned in the center of the stage behind the center table for the greatest effect.

Materials needed for set up on stage:
1. 20 inch (box) window fan
2. Long, extension cord for fan
3. Clear, wide tape
4. Microphone inside orbiter for the *Endeavor Landing Play*
5. Chair or other object to secure window fan from falling over
6. Stuffed or display astronaut – attached to a stand or dolly – **See Chapter 11 - Astronaut Display, page 142.**
7. Air Lock Box for the opening of orbiter – **See Chapter 5 – Building the Space Shuttle Orbiter, page 88.**

Mission Control Board – could be positioned on either side of stage for greatest effect.

Materials needed for set up on stage:
1. Extension cord for lights
2. Old, computer keyboard for effect
3. Wireless walkie-talkies for effect
4. Microphone for the *Endeavor Landing Play* – **See Chapter 9 – Mission Control Board, page 126.**

Table for Experiments – should be positioned in the center of the stage for greatest effect. The size of the table depends on how many experiments you are going to do in the production. One very large folding table should be adequate.

Materials needed for set up on stage:
1. Clear, wide tape
2. Large, folding table
3. Four, inflated balloons to use with the "matter experiments"

Blow the balloons up and store them under the table until it's time to use them.

4.   **SPACE, SCIENCE AND OTHER THINGS NAME OF SCHOOL**   Tape the **performance sign** to the front of the center table. The sign will also hide any boxes or extra equipment needed during the show. **See Chapter 12 - Performance Sign, page 149.**

5. Tape a trash bag to one side of the table for your trash during the show. Using the trash bag during the show will save clean-up time after the production (e.g., trash bag used for popped balloons, paper towels used to wipe up any spills of liquids). ***NOTE** - Be careful of whom you let help you clean up after the production. It's best if you clean the table yourself. After one of my previous shows, I had a mother come over to the table and without asking she just started throwing everything into the trash bag. The problem was that she threw away some of my needed supplies and my very long hatpin decorated with crepe paper that I use for the balloon experiments. She also threw away my strips of magic flash paper I use for chemical changes. Luckily, I was able to go back to the site the next day and by sifting through the trash, I retrieved my missing items.

6. Copies of the Student Scientific Quotes. **See Chapter 8 - Student Scientific Quotes, page 122.**

7. Set up all equipment for the other experiments on the center table (e.g., baking soda, vinegar, bowl of water, gas stove, Van De Graaf Generator).

8. Lay out the 12 air bags anywhere you can find room.

Chairs on Stage - If you are using your students in the production, you will need to arrange chairs for them on stage. Since the production will last about 1½ hours, the students will need to sit down when they are not performing their parts. Arrange the chairs on either side of the center table being careful not to block the path of the aliens.

Materials needed for set up on stage:

1. A chair for every student including the aliens
2. A chair or small table to hold the Tootsie Roll Pops or prizes given to audience volunteers - Place this chair away from everyone and make it easily accessible to the volunteers.
3. Two bags of Tootsie Roll Pops or prizes given to audience volunteers

• **Music** – Set the cassette/CD player where you can easily turn it on or off.

Materials needed for set up on stage:

1. Cassettes of the various songs
2. Extension/power strip for cassette player
3. Piano - if you can't find the cassette of the "Mission Control" song - **See Chapter 13 – Music, page 151.**

• **Balloon Race Experiment** – Find a spot on the wall six or seven feet above the ground to tie two, long pieces of string (e.g., attach the string to a pipe, a light fixture). Each string should be about 15 – 25 feet long. Tie one string to the spot you found on the wall and then tie the other string about three feet apart from the first one. **See Diagram 1.** Slide a straw onto each string. You will be attaching a balloon to the straw with scotch tape during the experiment. When the student blows up the balloon and releases it, the straw will allow the balloon to slide along the string. Last, cut a straw into three pieces and slide the pieces onto the end of the string. Form a triangle with the three pieces of straws and tie the end securely, so the first long straw doesn't fall off of the string and the triangle will be the place where the students will hold the string so the string doesn't slip out of their hands. **See Diagram 2.**

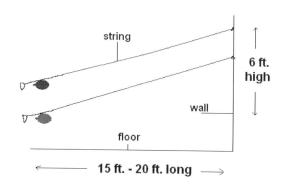

Diagram 1

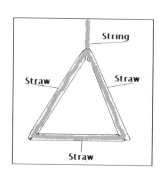

Diagram 2

Materials needed for set up on stage:

1. Ball of string
2. Scissors
3. Scotch tape
4. Four/five straws
5. Two, large balloons (Have extra balloons on hand incase some of them pop.) ***Note** – Make sure you lay the string down carefully after the set up so it won't tangle until you are ready to use it in the show. Make sure the students in the audience don't accidentally tangle the string before you are ready to use it in the show. Make sure the students hold on to the string when they release the balloons. I had one student let go of the string and balloon at the same time, and everything went flying. It was hilarious, but we had to start the experiment from the beginning.

Show Time

This section will follow the Show Manifest for the rest of the instructions. **See Chapter 1 – Show Manifest, page 1.** Manifest #1 is used with student participation, and Manifest #2 is used without student participation. Each manifest is an outline of the entire show listing acts and experiments…a quick reference guide to help you in remembering what comes next in the show or in other words a **"cheat sheet."** The manifest will become your right hand, so guard it carefully. As stated in Chapter 1, put the manifest into a clear page protector, and clip it to a clipboard for easy access.

Print out a copy of the show manifest, and follow along with the instructions below. As you read the instructions and follow the manifest, you will be able to better understand the premise of the production.

The morning of the show, have all participants including parent volunteers dress in their space gear. **See Chapter 7 – Space Camp T-Shirts, page 111 and Chapter 10 – Aliens, page 134.**

Right before the show, do a microphone and cassette/CD player check for sound quality and to correct any problems that might have developed during set up. A wireless microphone or headset microphone is ideal for you since it frees up your hands during the experiments. Two other microphones are needed (one inside the orbiter and one at the Mission Control Board).

Before the audience comes into the room or theater, have your classroom students performing in the *Endeavor Landing Play* go inside the orbiter so the audience won't see them. Have the aliens ready on the sidelines hidden from view. Alien masks are hot, so have the aliens flip the masks up on their foreheads to make it easier for them to breathe until it's their time to come on stage. When it's time for the aliens to appear, they can easily pull the masks down over their faces.

Have the two students at the Mission Control Board get ready for the show. Each student in the orbiter should have their own copy of the script with their name on it. Make sure a parent/volunteer stays inside the orbiter with them to help with behavior and to take care of the microphone. Have another parent/volunteer on stage, ready to open the air lock chamber when the students are ready to exit the orbiter. You can also open the air lock door yourself eliminating the need for a parent volunteer on stage. **See Chapter 5 – Building the Space Shuttle Orbiter, page 88.**

When the audience starts to file in, turn on the cassette song, "Theme from Star Wars." The music will set the mood for the space show. The music will also be a signal for the students in the orbiter, letting them know the audience is entering the room/theater and for them to be as quiet as possible. Turn off the music when everyone is seated and when you are ready for the show to begin.

Manifest

* Introduction – Rules for Presentation

When you are ready to begin the presentation have someone introduce you, or just say hello and introduce yourself. Tell the audience that they are going to have so much fun today and that they will participate in many exciting experiments, but before you start, you have to talk about the rules.

Hold up your hands in the "time-out" football signal. Tell the audience that this signal means to be quiet, to watch, and that it's your turn to talk. Tell them that sometimes the experiments will be really fun, and they will be yelling and screaming and that is O.K., but there will be times when they have to be quiet and listen for directions. Tell them that we are going practice the signal. Tell them to all start talking and watch for the signal.

When the students are all talking, hold up your hands in the "time-out" formation and see how fast they get quiet. Do this two more times. Tell them that you need about 55 volunteers from the audience, and you have instructed your students to only pick volunteers who are seated in their seats and are not screaming or yelling at them.

During all the times I have performed the show, I've had no disciplinary problems, because I have found that the students are so excited and stimulated. Teachers always tell me before the show that small children can't sit and be alert for 1½ hours, but I just smile and know that isn't true. Some of my performances have lasted for two hours, and the Kindergarten students were the best, remaining alert and participating the whole time while yelling for more. The production is very fast paced with lots of interaction with the crowd, so there is little time for them to be bored.

After you go over the rules for the production, create a key sentence that will signal the students waiting in the orbiter to start the play.

Say:

- "Look, the Endeavor is about to land. Let's listen. Take it away, Endeavor."

Point to the orbiter and walk to the side of stage.

* <u>Endeavor Landing Play</u>

See Chapter 6 – Landing of the Endeavor Script, page 98.

After the landing play the students will exit the orbiter one at a time. You will need to have a parent/teacher volunteer open the air lock chamber of the shuttle, or you can go over and do it yourself. The Commander will exit first. The students at the Mission Control Board will stand up as the students exit. The students will come out of the orbiter, walk to the center of the stage, stop, and salute Mission Control. The Mission Control students should be standing for the salute and return the salute. Have the student coming out of the orbiter walk over to his/her pre-assigned chair on stage and stand "at ease" (military at ease formation-hands behind back) facing the space ship and with his/her back to the audience. The students will wait until the entire crew has exited the orbiter before they sit down.

When all the students are standing at their chairs the Commander will yell, **"Attention!"** All the students will stand at attention – dropping their hands to their sides in a slapping motion. The Commander will yell, **"About face!"** All the students will turn clockwise and stand facing the audience. The Commander will yell, **"At Ease!"** The students will return to the "at ease stance" (with hands behind their backs). The Commander will yell, **"You may be seated!"** All students will then take their seats.

*Note – After the *Endeavor Landing Play*, have the parent helper inside the orbiter take the microphone out of the orbiter and place it into a microphone stand placed on the stage for the student readings. Make sure the microphone stand does not block the path of the aliens. After all the students are seated in their chairs you are ready to begin the magic tricks.

Materials needed for set up on stage:
1. A copy of the script for each student
2. Space shuttle orbiter
3. Two microphones (one in the shuttle and one on the Mission Control Board)
4. Parent/volunteer for inside the shuttle
5. Mission Control Board and keyboard
6. Chairs for each student
7. Table for the Mission Control Board
8. Optional – volunteer to open the shuttle air lock door

* *

* <u>Science is Magic - Magic Tricks</u>

To get the audience's attention very quickly, always start the show with magic. Everyone loves magic and it's great to see the smiles of amazement on the children's faces. Tell the audience that **"science is magic, or is it?"** Tell them you want to use the energy in the room to make a ball float so everyone has to concentrate and think about the ball floating in the air. You don't have to use the following magic tricks, or you can purchase what you want to use for the show depending on how much you want to spend.

*Note - See Chapter 4 - Magic Tricks, page 73 for details.

A. **Floating Ball (Trick #1)- *Note** - Before the show, set the trick up by attaching the ball to the micro fiber and wax. Then attach it to the back of the shuttle, out of the way of anyone tripping on the invisible micro fiber. While the students are coming out of the orbiter, you can walk off stage or go behind the orbiter and get set up for the first magic trick, the floating ball. The trick takes a minute to get the ball and string situated on your hand.

You can make anything float but try to find a small, plastic ball that is in two pieces like those plastic Easter eggs you can fill with candy. Using a bit of tacky wax (the kind that you stick papers onto walls of your bulletin boards) stick some wax on the inside of the ball, attach the micro fiber to the wax, and close the ball. (Try to find a small LCD light and a watch battery and make the ball light up so the audience can see it better.) Run the other end of the micro fiber over the top of your head, behind the back of your head, down your arm and attach the other end of the micro fiber to a ring on your finger using the tacky wax again. (Directions for this trick will come with the micro fiber.)

When you lift your arm, the ball will go down. When you move your head, the ball will follow the direction of your head. When you lower your arm, the ball will go up. The micro fiber is black and so thin that the audience won't see it. You can really make any small item seem to float. The students will be amazed. ***Note** - The audience will be able to see the fiber if you are too close to them and there is a lot of sunlight, otherwise the black fiber is invisible.

Materials needed for set up on stage:
1. Small object to make float (ball, dollar bill)
2. Micro fiber
3. Tacky-wax
4. Optional – LCD light and battery
* *

B. **Small LOTA BOWL (Trick # 2)** – In front of the audience, fill the bowl with water, and set it on the side of the stage. During various parts of the show, stop what you are doing and look over at the vase sitting on the stage. Slowly point to the vase, walk over to it and carry it over to an empty bucket also sitting on the stage. Dump out the water, and replace the vase to its original spot. About the third time you dump out the water, the audience will start to laugh and wonder where the extra water is coming from in the vase. You can dump water out of the vase about ten or twelve times before it's finally empty. Make a funny face when you stop to look over at the vase sitting on the stage. Students will laugh and think the situation is comical. Empty the bowl different times in the show.

Materials needed for set up on stage:

1. One, small Lota Bowl
2. Bucket

* *

C.   **Red Hanky (Trick #3)** — Wave a small, red hanky in front of the audience, and tell them that you will make it disappear. Pull up your sleeves to show that you are not holding anything. Put the fake thumb on one of your thumbs depending on whether you are right or left handed. Let's say you are right handed. Show the audience that you have nothing in your left hand by holding your left hand open, palm out. Holding the hanky over the fake thumb on your right hand, switch the hanky to your left hand and quickly wave your right hand at the audience making sure you point your fingers out to the audience so they don't notice that your right thumb is just a bit longer.

When you transfer the hanky back to your right hand, secretly take off the thumb and slip it into the palm of your left hand with the thumb opening face up. Your left palm closes over the fake thumb, and then begin to stuff the hanky into the hollow of the fake thumb resting in your left hand. Then for the last stuff, push your right thumb into the fake thumb. Hold it there and make the audience say the magic words, **school is cool,** and when you pull your hand up and then hold both hands up to the audience. The red hanky has disappeared.

The audience will yell and be amazed. You can then decide if you have ended the trick, or you can make the hanky reappear by putting the fake thumb back in your left hand and pulling out the hanky slowly from your left palm. On the last pull, make sure you slip the thumb back onto your right hand. Ask the audience to think about how you did the trick. You can keep your fake thumb and hanky in your pocket during the show, or place it on your center table for easy access.

Materials needed for set up on stage:
1. Red, silk hanky
2. Fake, hollow thumb
* *

D.   **Disappearing Mouse (Trick #4)** - One of my students gave me a small, squeaky, toy mouse for a gift. I always use this mouse for my shows. You can put any small toy into your disappearing bag. Hold up your toy and tell the audience you are going to make the toy disappear. Turn the bag upside down and show the audience that the bag is empty. Turn the bag inside out to show them that it's empty. Return the bag to its original position and drop the toy into the magic bag.

Have the audience say the magic words, **school is cool**, and while they are yelling, push the switch on the bag and the bag will move to its hidden, secret compartment. Turn the bag over and the toy will not fall out. Push the bag inside out and show the audience that the toy is really gone. Have the audience say the magic words again while pushing the switch and when you turn the bag over the toy falls out.

If you like, you can select a small student from the audience to help you with the trick...drop the toy inside of the bag and have the student look inside of it to verify to the audience that it has disappeared.

Materials needed for set up on stage:
1. Magic bag
2. Small toy or object to make disappear
3. Optional - 1 audience volunteer
* *

E.   **Color Changing Hanky (Trick #5)** - Or any other trick you might want to perform at this time. A blue and a green handkerchief are tied together. When you pull the hankies through your hand, they magically change to a red and a yellow handkerchief! When you repeat pulling them through your hand again, they change back to a blue and a green handkerchief. Can be repeated over and over instantly! The directions will come with the trick.

Materials needed for set up on stage:
1. Colored hankies
* *

F.   **Card in Orange Trick (Trick #6)** – You will need two decks of identical playing cards. **Before the show starts,** pick out a card from one deck, like the Ace of Hearts. Don't use that deck of cards anymore and discard the rest of the deck. Fold the Ace of Hearts into fourths and cut out one of the four sections and place that small section of the card on your center table for later use. Make sure you can see it on the table. Fold the remaining card (with the section missing out of it) and make a small cut in the bottom of an orange. Slide the folded card into the orange and place it over by the Mission Control board on a paper towel. Never go near the orange during the first part of the show.

Tell the audience that there is so much power in the room and so much knowledge, and we all know that knowledge is power. Tell them that we are going to use the power of **"telekinesis"** to make a card disappear and reappear inside the orange across the room.

Get a volunteer from the audience, usually a very small child who won't be able to see you fix the deck. While you are waiting for the volunteer to come up on stage, take the disappearing magic bag from the table and secretly put the ¼ section of the card (that you stored on your center table) into one section of the magic bag and flip the switch.

Hold a new deck of cards in your hand with your back slightly to audience and tell the child to tell you when to stop shuffling the cards. Always have the Ace of Hearts on the very bottom of the deck with your finger on it to prevent it from being shuffled. When the child says, stop, turn the deck over and give the Ace of Hearts to the child. Have the child hold it up to the audience.

Say:

• **"Your card is the Ace of Hearts."**

Have the child fold the card in half and then fold it in half again which makes fourths. Have the child tear it in half and then into fourths. Show the audience that the bag is empty and have the child look into the bag to verify that it's empty. Have the child drop all pieces of the cards into the disappearing bag. Flip the switch. Then have the students say the magic words, **school is cool**, and when you turn the bag over, only one piece of the card will fall out (the piece you cut out previously from the card in the orange). One little boy once told me, "Oops, you better try again."

Pretend to look shocked and puzzled. Walk over to the orange and using a sharp knife, very carefully cut the orange from the top. Smile and pull out the hidden card in the orange. When you open the card, one of the sections will naturally be missing. Then walk over to the stage, pick up the missing piece of card that fell out of your magic bag. Tell the audience that the trick almost worked, but you think some of the audience needs to stay in school to get more knowledge. It's an amazing trick. Good luck. ***Note** - the longer you keep the card in the orange, the more it will get wet and soggy. Put some plastic wrap around the card in the orange to keep it dry. You can easily cut the plastic wrap away with a knife.

Have the audience give the volunteer a round of applause and instruct the volunteer to select a lollipop when he/she leaves the stage.

Materials needed for set up on stage:
1. One orange (fruit)
2. Two of the exact same playing cards
3. Deck of cards
4. Sharp knife
5. Paper towels
6. Magic bag from magic trick #4
7. One, audience volunteer
8. Plastic wrap (optional)
* *

* <u>I've Got the Power - Music...D'Lite Thumbs</u>

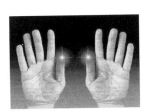

This is probably one of the highlights of the performance. Purchase three pairs of the thumb lights (each package has two thumbs) or purchase as many as you like depending on how much you want to spend. You will use two D'lite thumbs on stage and give the other four D'lite thumbs to teacher/parent volunteers planted in the audience. Keep the thumbs in your pocket or place them on your center table for easy access. Only give the volunteers one thumb each. ***Note** – rehearse the performance with the designated volunteers before the show to make sure they know how to use the thumb.

Ask the audience if there are any good dancers in the group.

<u>Have two of your classroom students select two volunteers each</u> <u>from the audience.</u> *Note – Ask the volunteers their names when they come up on stage.

Tell the audience that knowledge is power and turn on the music for the song, "I've Got the Power," by Snap that you have edited for the production. You can have a parent/teacher volunteer help you with the music and turn it on/off for you. Dance with the volunteers from the audience for about a minute.

With your D'lite thumbs in place, hold your hands over your head and start clapping and try to get the audience to clap to the music. Tell the audience that you can feel the power in the room and that on the count of three, you want them to hold their hands up and throw you the power. Tell the audience to put their hands up in the air and make a throwing motion for them to demonstrate how you want them to throw you the power.

Scream out the numbers:
- "1, 2, 3."

When the audience makes a throwing motion towards you, close your fingers and squeeze the D'lite thumbs to make the red lights come on as if you caught the power. Throw the power back to the audience. When you open your fingers the D'lite thumb lights will go out. Repeat the above procedure and light up your thumbs. This time call out one of the names of the person holding your fake thumb. Keep the lights burning on the thumbs.

Say:
- "Mrs. Smith (your volunteer's name), I'm going to throw you the power. Are you ready?"

Mrs. Smith answers you and you throw your hands out to her. Your light goes out and Mrs. Smith catches the power and makes her thumb light up.

Say:
- "Mrs. Smith, throw your power to Mr. Bojtos (your volunteer's name). Are you ready, Mr. Bojtos?"

Mr. Bojtos answers and Mrs. Smith throws the power to him. Her light goes out and Mr. Bojtos' thumb lights up. The procedure continues until the fourth person holding the fake thumb throws the light back to you. Throw it out to the audience. The students will usually yell at you to throw them the power.

When you select volunteers to dance from the audience, have some kind of reward for them for helping you with the experiments. Turn the music off. Have the audience give the volunteers a round of applause and instruct them to take one prize from the chair on the end of the stage as they leave. ***Note** – I purchased bags of Tootsie Roll Pop lollipops and kept them on a chair by the end of the stage. You can use pencils or any other prize you would like to give them.

Materials needed for set up on stage:
1. Three pairs of D'lite Magic Thumbs (6 thumbs total)
2. Music – cassette/CD player
3. Song – "I've Got the Power" by Snap
4. Four, audience parent/teacher volunteers (give each a thumb)
5. Four, audience volunteers (dancers)

* *

* <u>Knowledge is Power...Ping Pong Balls – Glow Ball</u>

Tell the audience that you are going to show them another demonstration of the power in the room.

Ask the audience:
- **"How many really smart people do we have here today? Raise your hands."**

<u>Have two of your students select two people each from the audience.</u> ***Note** – Ask the volunteers their names.

You can call more people up to the stage if you have more ping-pong balls. Position the volunteers in the center of the stage and give each of them a ping-pong ball. Tell them to hold the ball in their right hand and hold it up to the audience. Hold your "glow ball" which resembles a ping-pong ball in your right hand. Tell the audience that you are not smarter than them, but more educated since you have gone to college and we all know that knowledge is power.

Tell them that you are going to take some of the knowledge in your brain and make it travel down your arm and make your ping-pong ball light up. By touching the two metal strips on the "glow ball" simultaneously (which are positioned on the back of your ball and hidden by your fingers) your body will become a path for charged molecules and will complete a circuit and will make the ball glow brightly while making a funny, squeaky noise. When you release one of your fingers from one of the metal strips, the ball returns to normal. Pretend to concentrate very hard and make your "glow ball" light up. Tell the volunteers that it's now their turn to try and make their ping-pong balls light up.

Give them a moment and say:
- **"Look, I can make my ball light up so easily. I can make it light up this way, and that way. Try again."**

Put your hand holding the ball under your leg, put the ball behind your neck, or hold the ball up in the air and light it up. This will get the audience laughing.

When you are ready, call the volunteers over to you and take the ping-pong balls from them and put them on your table since you won't be using them anymore.

Show the audience your "glow ball" and tell them that it's not magic that made the ball light up, but a battery. Tell them that your body became the path for charged molecules. Explain that everything on Earth is made up of atoms. Atoms are the smallest particles on Earth. Atoms are recycled when living things die. The audience might have atoms in them that once belonged to dinosaurs. When two or more atoms join together, they make a molecule.

Tell them to think about a lamp. When the lamp is plugged into the wall socket and turned on, the electricity flows from the power plant to the lamp and makes it light up. In order for electricity to flow, there must be a continuous, conducting path between the negative pole and the positive pole of the power source (electrical outlet). When the lamp is turned on, the electrical path is called a **closed circuit** (a circuit with no gaps in it). Current flows from the positive side of the power source (the electrical outlet) to the loads (light bulb) wired into the circuit and back to the negative side of the power source. The molecules can flow freely. When the lamp is turned off, the path of the molecules is interrupted and that's called an **open circuit.** A broken wire or an "open" (off) switch both leave gaps in a circuit preventing electrons from traveling from one side of the power source to the other. Thus, electrons will not flow.

Have the volunteers hold hands and form a circle. Have the student closest to you put one of his/her fingers on one of the metal tabs on the "glow ball." Put your finger on the other tab. Tell the student not to touch you, only the metal tab. When you hold hands with the student on your other side, the ball will light up and squeak. That is an example of a closed circuit. When you let one of the student's hands go, the ball will return to normal, showing an example of an open circuit. Have everyone hold hands again and the ball will light up. Keep holding onto the students' hands and select another student in the circle to let go of the circle. The ball will stop. ***Note** – The principle can be demonstrated with about 24 students holding hands in the circle.

Pick one student to come to the front of the stage. Have the student put his/her finger on the metal strip on the "glow ball," being careful not to touch any part of you. With one of your fingers on the other metal tab, touch the student's nose. The ball will light up. Touch the student's ear. The ball will light up. Touch the student's elbow. The ball will light up. Have the audience give the volunteers a round of applause and instruct the volunteers to select a lollipop when they leave the stage.

Materials:
1. Glow Ball
2. Four, ping-pong balls

* *

* <u>Chemical/Physical Changes...Magic Paper</u>

Tell the audience you want to talk about Chemical and Physical Changes. Tell them in nature all living things have three major elements in them, **Oxygen, Carbon and Hydrogen.**

Ask the audience:
- **"What element does your body need when you breathe air into your body?"** (Answer: Oxygen)
- **"What element do you breathe out of your body?"** (Answer: Carbon Dioxide)

Tell the audience that you want to talk about:

Physical Changes - Say to the audience:

- "Let's talk about physical changes. In science, a physical change is a change that makes something look different, but you still have the same substance or have the same thing."
- "You can even add things to the experiment, but you will still have the same substance."
- "If I gained fifty pounds, would I look different?" (Wait for the audience to yell yes after each question.)
- "Would it still be me?"
- "If I dyed my hair black, would I look different?"
- "Would it still be me?"
- "If I had plastic surgery on my face, would I look different?"
- "Would it still be me?"
- "If I went to the moon and my butt got really big, would I look different?"
- "Would it still be me?"
- "Those are examples of a physical change."
- "What kind of change?" (Wait for the audience to yell physical change.)

Hold up a sheet of white paper and ask the students in the audience to describe it to you (e.g., smooth, white, rectangle). Crumple the paper up in your hand and open it. The paper will be all wrinkled. Ask the audience to describe it to you again.

Ask:

- "Does the paper look different?"
- "Is it still paper?"

Color the paper with a magic marker.
Ask:

- "Does the paper look different?"
- "Is it still paper?"

Tear the crumpled paper in half.
Ask:

- "Does the paper look different?"
- "Is it still paper?"

Tear the paper in half again.
Ask:

- "Does the paper look different?"
- "Is it still paper?"

Tell the audience that those were examples of physical changes.

Chemical Changes - Say to the audience:

- "Let's talk about chemical changes. In science, a chemical change is a change that when you add something to the substance it turns the substance into something totally different. You will have a new substance."

- "Everyone say, chemical change."

- "I'm going to show you an experiment that is dangerous. I need you to hold up your right hand and repeat after me."

*Note – Turn your back to the audience and hold up your right hand to show the smaller students the correct hand to hold up.

Say:
- "I promise,"
- "I will not try this experiment at home."

Tell the audience you have special chemicals and supplies that they don't have, so they can't do the same experiment, and they might get hurt if they play with fire at home.

Using a lighter, ignite one of the pieces of paper and watch it burn for a second and blow out the flame. Have a bowl of water on your table incase you need to put out the fire.

Tell the audience:
- "The Oxygen and Hydrogen are burning off and you have this black substance left on the paper. It's called Carbon."

Ask:
- "Does the paper look different?"
- "Do you still have paper? No, you have a new substance called ash."

Crumble off some of the ash in your fingers to show the audience that it's very soft and isn't the same paper. Hold up a piece of magic flash paper. Ask the audience to describe it to you again. A very small piece (4 in. x 1 in.) is all that is needed, or you can use a larger piece and make your flame as large as you want.

Tell the audience:
- "I want to show you another chemical change. Watch closely and see if you can find the carbon."

Ignite the piece of magic flash paper using a cigarette lighter, and throw it into the air. The paper will burn off so fast that it will completely disappear. The audience will be amazed. Do it about three more times

Ask:

- **"Where is the Carbon?"**
- **"What kind of change was that?"** (Answer: Chemical change)

Proceed to tell the audience that you have a special magic paper that magicians use in their magic acts. The paper is treated with highly flammable chemicals that make it so hot that disappears completely when ignited (burned). Sometimes science is used for magic.

Materials:
1. Sheet of 8 in. x 11 in. white paper
2. Cigarette lighter
3. Magic marker
4. Small strips of magic paper (4 in. x 1 in.)
5. Large bowl of water (to put out fire if needed)
* *

* <u>Mission: Knowledge is Power</u>
* <u>Aliens</u>

It's now time for the hidden aliens to make their entrance. **See Chapter 10 – Aliens, page 134.** It's a good idea to have two parent helpers' stay with the aliens and cue them on when to run out around the orbiter. Give each parent/teacher helper a copy of the show manifest so they will be able to watch for the times that the aliens are needed on stage. You should have "key words" for the aliens to listen for and know when to come out.

Say to the audience:

- **"My mission here today is to tell you that knowledge is power."**

Yell the words, **mission** and **knowledge is power**, really loud and when the aliens hear you say the words, **mission and knowledge is power, in a yelling voice** that would be the cue for them to run out. The word, **mission**, is the major cue word.

The alien, **Goo-Goo**, comes out first carrying sign #1 that

Me Alien

says "Me Alien." Put large numbers on the backs of the signs so the alien, **Goo-Goo**, knows which sign to take out each trip. Once the alien, **Goo-Goo**, has used sign #1, he/she should get ready with sign #2 and then sign #3. ***Note** – Remember to place the signs in an easy place for the aliens to find.

Holding the sign so the audience can read it, the alien, **Goo-Goo**, quickly walks from one side of the stage to the other waving to the audience. ***Note** – Make sure the path is clear for the aliens to walk through. Tape all electrical wires down to the floor. Leave enough room between the orbiter and the center table for them to easily walk through. The masks make it a bit difficult for the aliens to see, so the path must be clear. The aliens will walk in between the orbiter and the center table. Make sure you are in front of the center table talking to the audience when the aliens come out.

Usually, the first time the audience sees the alien, they don't know what to expect and they are a bit quiet and will wait to see what the alien does. When they see that the alien is going off the stage they will start yelling at you to look behind you and notice the alien.

When you are sure the alien, **Goo-Goo**, is off the stage, slowly turn around and check behind you. Face the audience again.

Say:
- **"What are you talking about? I don't see anything!"**

When you are facing the audience, the alien, **Me Too**, comes out and walks in the same path as the alien, **Goo-Goo**.

The alien, **Me Too**, will carry a sign that says, **Me Too**.

Me Too

The alien, **Me Too**, only has one sign to carry each time. The alien also waves to audience and quickly disappears off stage. The audience will yell a bit louder for you to turn and see the alien. Again you turn around and don't see any aliens. The audience will start screaming, **"Alien! Alien!"**

Say:
- **"What are you talking about?"**

27

- "I don't see anything!"
- "There are no such things as aliens."
- "You must be seeing things."

Act normal and go on to the next part of the production.

Materials:
1. Two students dressed as aliens
2. Sign that says, "Me Alien"
3. Sign that says, "Me Too"
4. Hiding place for the aliens (stage, or two folding screens)
* *

Group A - Student Scientific Quotes
(Omit if not using students)

Call out the names of your classroom students in Group A to come up to the microphone to do their student readings. Hand out the student copies of the readings that you are holding on the side of the center table. **See Chapter 8 - Student Scientific Quotes, page 122.** Have each student state their name and read their card. Take the cards from the students when they are finished and instruct them to be seated.

Materials:
1. Cards with student readings on them
2. Microphone
* *

* Matter...balloons

Say to the audience:
- "Everything on Earth is made up of matter."
- "Everyone say the word, matter."
- "A very simple definition of matter is - something that takes up space, has weight and occurs in solid, liquid, or gas form."
- "Is the table matter?" (Answer: Yes)
- "Yes, because it's taking up space on the stage and I can weigh it to see how heavy it is. It is a solid."
- "Is the space ship matter?" (Answer: Yes)
- "Yes, it's taking up space and I can weigh it. It's a solid."
- "Am I matter?" (Answer: Yes)
- "Yes, very good."
- "Is air matter?"

This is the spot where the audience will experience confusion. Half of the audience will yell yes and the other half will yell no.

Ask:

- "How many people think air is matter? Please raise your hands."
- "How many people think air is not matter? Please raise your hands."

Take out one of the inflated balloons that are stored under the center table. Hold the balloon up to the audience.

Say:

- "I have a balloon."
- "What's inside of the balloon?" (The audience will answer – air.)
- "Is the air inside of the balloon taking up space inside of the balloon?"
- "If I had a small scientific scale, could I weigh it and find out how much it weighs?"
- "What is air, a solid, liquid or gas?" (Answer: Gas)
- "O.K., I would like to ask you again. Is air matter?" (The audience should yell, yes.)

Materials:
1. One, inflated balloon
****

* Balloon Pop with a Pin
Have one of your students select one person from the audience.

*Note – Before the show, tape some streamers of colored crepe paper to the top of the hatpin so it will make it easier for the audience to see your hatpin. Introduce the volunteer to the audience. Get a hatpin off of your center table.

Say:

- "I have a hatpin, a big hatpin."
- "What would happen if I stuck this hatpin inside of this balloon?" (The audience should tell you it would pop.)
- "Exactly, it will pop. The popping sound you hear when a balloon pops is the air inside of the balloon, rushing out so fast that it makes a huge noise ripping open the balloon."

Demonstrate by popping the balloon. Pop another balloon. Get a third balloon.

Say:

- "I am going to show you how you can stick this pin inside of a balloon and it won't pop."

Have the audience volunteer hold the balloon for you while you put the scotch tape on it.

Say:

- "Take about three strips of scotch tape and criss-cross it in one spot making a star out of the scotch tape." See Diagram 3. *Note – Tape the balloon as you are talking.

   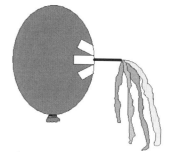

Diagram 3   Diagram 4

- "The scotch tape will hold the sides of the balloon together and the air will not be able to rush out of the balloon with a pop."
- "Is everyone ready? Say the magic words, school is cool."

Take the balloon from the audience helper incase the balloon pops and the pin flies, hurting the volunteer. Slowly push the pin through the center of the tape. The pin should slide into the balloon and not pop.

Say to the volunteer:

- "Is the pin inside of the balloon?" (The volunteer should respond, yes.)

Hold the balloon up for the audience to see. **See Diagram 4**. ***Note** – Depending on the quality of the balloon, the pin should stay in the balloon until all of the air leaks out of the balloon. I have had balloons pop even with the tape holding the sides together, so tell the students the experiment might work and it might not work. After holding up the balloon and showing the audience the hatpin is inside of the balloon (remove your hand from the hatpin and let the audience see the hatpin with the crepe paper streamers being suspended by the balloon). Make sure you hold the balloon away from the volunteer incase the balloon pops. Take the pin out and tell the audience you will show them that the balloon will really pop if you stick the pin in any other place than the where the tape is holding the sides together. Have the volunteer pop the balloon. Have the audience give the volunteer a round of applause and instruct the volunteer to select a lollipop when he/she leaves the stage.

Materials:
1. Four, inflated balloons (incase one pops before needed)
2. Large hatpin with strips of crepe paper attached to the top
3. Roll of scotch tape
* *

* Acids/Bases – Vinegar and Baking Soda

Tell the audience you want to talk about acids and bases. Some substances in nature are acids and some substances are bases. Acids are strong substances while bases are mild substances. If a substance is in-between an acid and a base, it's called neutral.

Say:
- **"What do you think a lemon would be, acid or base?"** (Answer: acid)
- **"Good."**
- **"In nature, you can't mix an acid and a base together without making a chemical reaction."**

Hold up a bottle of vinegar. Tell the audience that vinegar is sour, and it's an acid. Show the audience a box of baking soda and tell them that baking soda is mild and is a base. ***Note** – Demonstrate to the audience while you are talking. Have a large tray on your center table to catch the spilled liquid and powder.

Put about two inches of vinegar into a clear glass. Tell the audience to watch what happens when you add the baking soda. Drop two heaping teaspoons of baking soda into the glass and stir. The chemical reaction happens immediately, and it makes Carbon Dioxide gas.

31

Say:

- "I see the mixture is bubbling and making Carbon Dioxide gas."
- "What gas do we breathe out when we breathe?"
- "Right, Carbon Dioxide gas."
- "Now let's see if we can catch the gas in the chemical reaction."

In front of the audience, pour about two inches of vinegar into a clear wine bottle. Put about two heaping teaspoons of baking soda into a very large balloon. Place the balloon opening over the opening of the wine bottle being careful not get any baking soda into the wine bottle at this point. Just let the balloon fall over the side of the wine bottle. **See Diagram 5.**

Diagram 5

Tell the audience that in order for the trick to work, they have to say the new magic words, **OONA – Spoona- Big Balloon-na.**

Say:

- "I will count, 1, 2, 3, and you will yell, **OONA – Spoona- Big Balloon-na. Are you ready?"**
- "1, 2, 3."

Let the audience yell and don't do anything. Shake your head "no."

Say:

- "Is that all the louder you can say it?"
- "Let's try it again."
- "1, 2, 3."

Have the audience yell the magic words again and do not do anything. Just shake your head "no" again. Look sad.

Say:
- "Nothing happened. This is your last time, so really yell, **OONA – Spoona- Big Balloon-na.**"
- "1, 2, 3."

The students will outdo themselves this time and will yell pretty loud. While they are yelling, lift the edge of the balloon up and dump the baking soda into the bottle and watch the chemical reaction blow the balloon up.

Say:
- "**Great job. Look, in the first experiment, we saw the bubbles of the gas. This time we caught the gas. Now let's see the force of the gas.**"
- "**Listen when I take the balloon off of the bottle. You will hear a little passing gas noise.**"

Go over to the standing microphone so the audience will be able to hear, and slowly lift the edge of the balloon off of the bottle. You will hear a little burp. The students always love that noise…sounds like passing gas.

Place the bottle and balloon on the table and get the other empty wine bottle. Pour about two inches of vinegar into the bottle. ***Note** – before the show, grease the inside of the opening of the wine bottle with Vaseline to make it a bit easier for the cork to fly off the bottle. Also before the show, attach some streamers of crepe paper to the cork so the students will be able to watch the cork fly across the room. You can use a thumbtack to attach the streamers or tape or glue. **See Diagram 6.**

Diagram 6

Ask the audience:
- "**How do you think I can get the baking soda into the wine bottle and put this cork on it before the chemical reaction happens?**"

(Answer: Make a paper bullet out of Kleenex small enough to fit into the opening of the bottle.)

Choose students in the audience to give you the answer to the question. They will tell you to pour the baking soda into the bottle fast. But tell them that as soon as the baking soda hits the vinegar, the reaction will start and you want to capture "all" of the gas because you want to measure the force of the gas and if some of the gas leaks out, your experiment won't be accurate.

If no one guesses the correct answer, tell the audience you are going to make a paper bullet out of a piece of Kleenex.

Cut a 2 in. X 4 in. section piece out of one sheet of Kleenex. Place two teaspoons (or as much as you can) on the cut out tissue. Fold the sides over and roll into a bullet shape. Tilt the bottle sideways a bit, and slide the bullet into the opening of the bottle making sure the bullet stays in the top, narrow opening. **See Diagram 7.**

Diagram 7   **Diagram 8**

Keeping the bottle at an angle carefully put the cork on top of the wine bottle. Do not make it so tight that the cork won't be able to fly off. **See Diagram 8.** Aim the bottle away from audience to a place where the cork can travel about thirty feet without damaging anything. Make sure the audience will be able to see the cork fly.

When you are in position, tilt the bottle upright so the paper bullet will fall into the vinegar. Tilt the bottle back to the above angle and shake the bottle up and down to help mix the baking powder and vinegar. The cork will make a huge popping sound and fly off about thirty feet.

Tell the audience that now you have seen the force of the bottle.

Materials:
1. Clear, tall glass
2. Bottle of vinegar

3. Box of baking soda
4. Tray to the catch mess from the experiments
5. Paper towels or rags
6. Two, clear, wine bottles
7. One cork with crepe paper streamers
8. Jar of Vaseline
9. Balloon
10. Teaspoon
11. One tissue (Kleenex)
12. Scissors

* *

* <u>Mission: Knowledge is Power</u>
* <u>Aliens</u>

It's time for the hidden aliens to make their second appearance. **See Chapter 10 – Aliens, page 134.**

Say to the audience:

- **"My mission here today is to tell you that knowledge is power."**

   Yell the words, **mission** and **knowledge is power**, really loud and when the aliens hear you say the words, **mission and knowledge is power, in a yelling voice** that would be the cue for them to run out. The word, **mission**, is the major cue word.

   The alien, **Goo-Goo**, comes out first carrying sign #2

ALIENS RULE

that says "Aliens Rule."

   Holding the sign so the audience can read it, the alien, **Goo-Goo**, quickly walks from one side of the stage to the other waving to the audience.

   When the audience sees the alien, this time they will start yelling at you to look behind you and notice the alien.

   When you are sure the alien, **Goo-Goo**, is off the stage, slowly turn around and check behind you. Face the audience again.

Say:

• **"What are you talking about? I don't see anything!"**

When you are facing the audience, the alien, **Me Too**, comes out and walks in the same path as the alien, **Goo-Goo**.

The alien, **Me Too**, will carry a sign that says, **Me Too**.

> **Me
> Too**

The alien, Me Too, also waves to audience and quickly disappears off stage. The audience will yell a bit louder for you to turn and see the alien. Again you turn around and don't see any aliens. The audience will start screaming, "Alien! Alien!"

Say:

• **"What are you talking about?"**
• **"I don't see anything!"**
• **"I told you already, there are no such things as aliens."**
• **"You must be seeing things. I don't see anything."**

Act normal and go on to the next part of the production.

Materials:
1. Two aliens
2. Sign that says, "Aliens Rule"
3. Sign that says, "Me Too"
4. Hiding place for the aliens (stage, or two folding screens)

* *

Group B - Student Scientific Quotes

(Omit if not using students)

Call out the names of your classroom students in Group B to come up to the microphone to do their student readings. Hand out the student copies of the readings that you are holding on the side of the center table. **See Chapter 8 - Student Scientific Quotes, page 122.** Have each student state their name and read their card. Take the cards from the students when they are finished and instruct them to be seated.

Materials:
1. Cards with student readings on them
2. Microphone

* *

* Air Bags

While Group B students are reading their scientific quotes – **Have six of your students select two people each from the audience.** (Have your students select some adults or people with a lot of **hot air.**)

Line up the twelve volunteers across the center stage and give each one of them an air bag. Tell the audience you are going to have the volunteers make a **"hypothesis, or their best guess"** as to how many breaths of air it will take them to blow up the air bag.

Go to each volunteer. Ask them for their name and ask them:
- **"How many breaths of air do you think it will take you to blow up this air bag?"**

When everyone has given you their estimate, say to the audience:
- **"On the count of three, we are going to have the volunteers blow up their bags, and we will count how many breaths of air it will take them. Is everyone ready? 1, 2, 3."**

Count to about ten breaths and say:
- **I think that's enough. Does anyone want to change their hypothesis or guess?"**

Go back through the line of twelve volunteers and ask them if they want to change their hypothesis?

Say:
- **"What if I told you that I could blow up the air bag in one breath?"**

The audience and the volunteers on stage will usually make noises to disagree with you.

*Note – Everyone who has ever tried to blow up the air bag has always put the air bag up to his/her mouth to inflate the bag. See the pictures on the next page. The trick of the air bag is to hold the air bag at least 12 inches from your mouth and blow.

Say:

- "If I blow up the air bag in one breath, then you have to promise me that you will make an "A" on your next Science test. O.K?"

- "In 1738, a man named, David Bernoulli, did some experiments with high and low air pressure. He invented the Bernoulli Principle. When you blow the air in front of you into the bag, you create a low pressure and all of the surrounding air will follow your breath into the air bag because Mother Nature loves balance or for everything to be equal."

- "I want you to think of your father's foot or a 12 inch ruler."

- "Hold the air bag away from your mouth about 12 inches or think of your father's foot in front of your mouth." (The audience will usually yell, "Ugh.")

- "Watch me. Take a big breath of air and blow into the bag, holding the bag about 12 inches from your mouth and then quickly grab the bag shut."

At this time ask one of the students on stage to hold the end of your bag.

Say:

- "I never said you couldn't have help."

Make sure all of the air is out of the bag. Pull the bag tight and hold your hands around the opening of the bag. Holding the air bag 12 inches from your mouth, blow into the bag and quickly shut the bag after it inflates.

Have all the twelve volunteers get a partner to hold the end of the bag. Use your students sitting on stage to help hold the ends of the bags for the audience volunteers. Have them take all of the air out of the bag. **See the picture on the next page.**

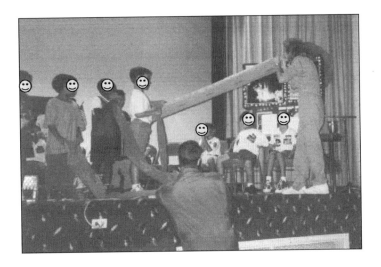

Say:

- "We are going to count to three and when we say three, everyone blow up your bag."
- "Remember to pull the bag tight, blow into the bag and quickly shut the bag after it inflates."
- "Are you ready? 1, 2, 3."

After the volunteers blow up the bags have the audience give them a round of applause and tell the volunteers to please take a lollipop on their way off of the stage. ***Note** – Please tell the students not to pop the air bags once they have them filled with air. Some of my volunteers squeezed the bags and made holes in them. If that happens, clear, wide tape will fix the damage and the air bag will be as good as new.

Materials:
1. Twelve, air bags (or as many as you purchase)
* *

Group C - Student Scientific Quotes
(Omit if not using students)

Call out the names of your classroom students in Group C to come up to the microphone to do their student readings. Hand out the student copies of the readings that you are holding on the side of the center table. **See Chapter 8 - Student Scientific Quotes, page 122.** Have each student state their name and read their card. Take the cards from the students when they are finished and instruct them to be seated.

Materials:
1. Cards with student readings on them
2. Microphone

* *

* Sound Vibrations - Chicken Cups

While Group C students are reading their scientific quotes - **Have six of your students select two people each from the audience**.

Line up the twelve volunteers across the center stage and give each one of them a chicken cup.

Materials:
1. Six, small, plastic cups (red/blue type) **See Diagram 9.**
2. Six, large, plastic cups (red/blue type) **See Diagram 10.**
3. Scissors

4. Ball of string
5. Sharp object to poke a hole in the cup (compass works great)
   See Diagram 11.
6. Bag of sponges (for washing dishes or cars)

Diagram 9

6 Small cups

Diagram 10

6 Large cups

Diagram 11

Compass

Directions for Making Chicken Cups:

1. Turn the cup upside down. Using the sharp edge of the compass, make two holes in the bottom of the cup. Make a larger hole in the center of the cup big enough for the string to pass through and make a smaller hole along the edge of the cup to let air pass through. **See Diagram 12.**

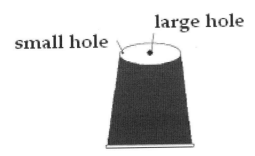

small hole   large hole

Diagram 12

2. Cut a piece of string 4 ft. long.

3. Thread one end of the string through the hole in the bottom center of the cup and make a large knot. The knot should be on the outside of the cup. Make sure the knot is secure so that when you pull on the string, the knot will not pass through the hole. **See Diagram 13.**

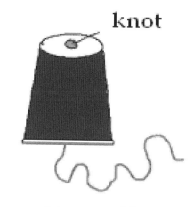

Diagram 13

4. Cut out a 2 in. x 4 in. section from a sponge. **See Diagram 14.**

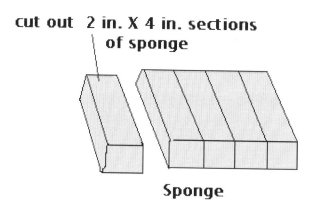

Diagram 14

5. Tie the piece of sponge to the other end of the string on the cup making sure the string is tied to the middle of the sponge. **See Diagram 15.**

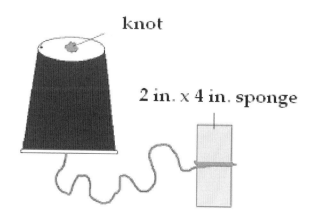

Diagram 15

6. Repeat steps **1 - 5** to make eleven more chicken cups.

7. Before using the cups on stage, wet the sponge and wring out any excess water.

8. To store the cups for transport, roll the string around the sponge and place the sponge inside of the cup. The cups can then be stacked on top of each other.

   Tell the volunteers to put their cups on the floor and to follow your directions.

Say:
- "I want to talk about sound waves. Everyone say, sound waves."
- "A wave can be described as a disturbance that travels through something (e.g., water, air, metal) transporting energy from one location to another."
- "How many people have ever thrown a stone out into water causing waves to go out through the water? Raise your hands."
- "How many people have ever played with a slinky and when you pulled on it, made the slinky wave back and forth?"
- "A sound wave is similar in nature to a slinky wave. I will show you the slinky later on and we will test for waves."
- "Sound travels in a straight path but in waves, big waves, little waves, long waves."
- "Sound will move at the same speed, about 330 meters per second, but the shorter the wavelength, the higher sound; the longer the wavelength, the lower the sound."

| High-frequency Sound Wave | Low-Frequency Sound Wave |

- "Say, vibration. When something makes a sound or vibration, your ears act like radio receivers and pick up that sound or vibration."
- "How many of you have ever sat close to the TV or stereo speakers and the sound has been so loud that you actually could feel the vibrations in your chest?"
- "My ears stuck out so bad when I was little the other kids would make fun of me. They called me Dumbo ears."

- "I used to feel bad about having big ears, but not anymore, because since my ears stick out, they pick up more sound vibrations."
- "I want everyone to hold your hands up in the air. Cup your hands like you are going swimming through the water."
- "Watch me do this first before you try it so you will know what to do."
- "When I say, 1, 2, 3, you will all say, LAAAAAAAAAAAAAAAA, and as you are holding that note, slowly put your hands behind your ears, making Mickey Mouse ears. The sound should get louder as you put your hands closer to your ears and be really loud when your hands are behind your ears. Let me try it first, watch."

Say the word "LA" and hold the note while putting your cupped hands behind your ears.

Say:

- "O.K. Hands in the air. Cup them like you are swimming. 1, 2, 3, LAAAAAAAAAAAAAAAA."

Have the students do it one more time to make sure everyone has the chance to do it correctly.

Say:

- "Great job. Now we are going to have our volunteers pretend they are chickens."
- "Please pick up the cups and hold the sponge in the hand that you write with. Put the cup into the other hand."
- "Hold the cup upside down with the string hanging out of it. Hold the cup tightly so that if you pulled on the string, the cup won't fall out of your hand."
- "With your other hand, fold the sponge in half like a little duck's beak. Hold the sponge so you can make it open and close."
- "I want the people with the small cups to step forward. You will try the experiment first."
- "Let me demonstrate first. I will put my sponge around the string towards the top of the cup and squeeze really hard. I will then pull downwards with small strokes squeezing as I am pulling."

*Note – the vibrations from pulling on the string will make sounds exactly like a chicken squawking. **See Diagram 16.**

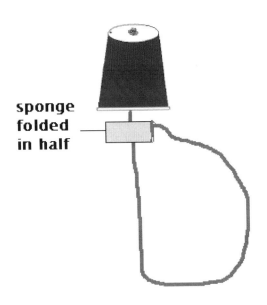

sponge folded in half

Diagram 16

Say:

- "Ready, 1, 2, 3."

Let the volunteers squawk for a few moments. Tell them to stop and step back for a minute. Bring up the next six volunteers with the larger cups.

Say:

- "I want everyone to listen to the sound of the big cups to see if there is a difference in the sound from the smaller cups."
- "Ready, 1, 2, 3."

Let the volunteers squawk for a few moments.

Say:

- "Did you notice a different sound?"
- "Small cups, please squawk. Stop, big cups squawk. Now everybody squawk."

While they are squawking, make some dance moves on stage. The audience will laugh. Have the volunteers stop and tell the audience to give them a round of applause.

Thank them and tell them that they may keep the cups if they promise not to squawk them during the remainder of the performance. Remind them to take a lollipop for helping.

* *

Group D - Student Scientific Quotes
(Omit if not using students)

Call out the names of your classroom students in Group D to come up to the microphone to do their student readings. Hand out the student copies of the readings that you are holding on the side of the center table. **See Chapter 8 - Student Scientific Quotes, page 122.** Have each student state their name and read their card. Take the cards from the students when they are finished and instruct them to be seated.

Materials:
1. Cards with student readings on them
2. Microphone

* *

* Shuttle Telephone...Sound Vibrations
http://www.slinkytoys.com/catalog/cat2/catalog.asp?action=catv&cat id=33

While Group D students are reading their scientific quotes - **Have one of your students select two people from the audience.**

Continuing with the experiments on sound have your two audience volunteers hold a slinky and pull it, but not too tight. Tell the audience to watch for the wave in the slinky as one of the volunteers makes a small jerking motion in the slinky. The other volunteer should hold his or her end of the slinky still.

A wave is produced traveling the entire length of the slinky, echoing or bouncing from one end to the other and back again.

The wave will bounce from one person to the other and continue to go back and forth until it stops. Remind the audience that sound travels like the waves in the slinky, in a straight line, but in waves.

Space Telephone – Laser Sounds
Materials:
1. Slinky
2. Two, empty, large, coffee cans
3. Pliers
4. Hammer
5. Nail

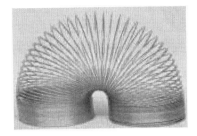

Make a space telephone out of a metal slinky and two empty coffee cans.

Directions for Making the Space Telephone:
1. Using a hammer and the nail, make a hole in the center of both coffee cans. **See Diagram 17.**

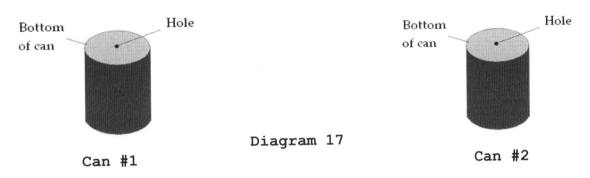

Bottom of can   Hole   Bottom of can   Hole

Diagram 17

Can #1   **Can #2**

2. Using the pair of pliers, insert one end of the metal slinky into the hole and bend the wire inside the can so the slinky doesn't pull out of the hole. Do the same to the other can. **See Diagram 18.**

Diagram 18

Place a chair in the center of the stage. Borrow one of your students' chairs from on stage. Have the two volunteers stand on either side of the chair and pull the slinky tight, but not too tight. Ask one of the volunteers to swing the coffee can out and make the slinky hit the side of the chair. The effect will be an amazing laser gun sound. Hold your microphone near one of the coffee cans. The coffee can will amplify the vibrations from the slinky. The sound will have a hollow effect sounding very much like something from outer space.

Have the audience give the volunteer a round of applause and instruct the volunteer to select a lollipop when he/she leaves the stage.

The experiment doesn't have much scientific benefit, but the students always seem to love the sound effects and will write about it in their final paper as one of their favorite parts of the show.

* *

* <u>Mission: Knowledge is Power</u>
* <u>Aliens</u>

It's time for the hidden aliens to make their final appearance. **See Chapter 10 – Aliens, page 134** for specific details.

Say to the audience:

- **"My mission here today is to tell you that knowledge is power."**

Yell the words, **mission** and **knowledge is power**, really loud and when the aliens hear you say the words, **mission and knowledge is power, in a yelling voice** that would be the cue for them to run out. The word, **mission**, is the major cue word.

The alien, **Goo-Goo**, comes out first carrying sign #3 that

TAKE ME
TO YOUR
LEADER

says "Take me to your leader."

Holding the sign so the audience can read it, the alien, **Goo-Goo**, quickly walks from one side of the stage to the other waving to the audience.

When the audience sees the alien again, they will start yelling at you to look behind you and notice the alien.

When you are sure the alien, **Goo-Goo**, is off the stage, slowly turn around and check behind you. Face the audience again.

Say:

- **"What are you talking about? I don't see anything! I keep telling you, I don't see any aliens. "**

When you are facing the audience, the alien, **Me Too**, comes out and walks in the same path as the alien, **Goo-Goo**. The alien, **Me Too**, will carry a sign that says, **Me Too**.

Me
Too

The alien, Me Too, also waves to audience. The alien, Goo Goo, reappears and both aliens drop their signs and slowly creep over to you with their hands up in the air in a scary fashion. Shake your head "no" to the crowd and ignore them. The roar of the crowd will be incredible. The aliens will come over to you and tap you on the shoulders.

When you feel the taps, turn around and scream. Act scared and jump out of the way. Follow the script below holding the microphone under the aliens' mouth when it's their turn to talk so the audience can hear them through the masks.

See the following script:

Teacher to Goo Goo:	"**Who are you?**"
Goo Goo:	"Goo Goo."
Teacher to audience:	"Goo Goo?"
Teacher to Goo Goo:	"**Where are you from, Goo Goo?**"
Goo Goo:	"Goo Gone."
Teacher to audience:	"Goo Gone?"
Teacher to Me Too:	"**What's your name?**"
Me Too:	"**Me Too.**"

Teacher to audience:	"Me Too."
Teacher to Me Too:	"And are you from Goo Gone?"
Me Too:	"Me Too."
Teacher to aliens:	"What do you want? Why are you here?"
Goo Goo:	"I want the power!"
Me Too:	"Me Too."

Have a parent/volunteer turn on the cassette to the song, "I've Got the Power," by Snap. The aliens will start dancing.

After the aliens dance around for a minute, say:
- **"Get out of here. You can't have our power. Shoo! Get off my stage and quit bothering us. Shoo, Get!"**

Get the aliens off of the stage in a shooing motion. The aliens should go backstage, change out of the costumes and join your other classroom students on stage. Remember during your stage set up to add two chairs for the aliens.

Materials:
1. Two aliens
2. Sign that says, "Take Me To Your Leader"
3. Sign that says, "Me Too"
4. Hiding place for the aliens (stage, or two folding screens)
* *

* <u>Forces — Centrifugal Force - Bucket of Water</u>

Take the bucket of water filled with the water from the Lota Bowl and say:

- **"What would happen if I held this bucket of water upside down over my head?"** (The audience should tell you the water would fall out on your head.)
- **"Everyone say, centrifugal force."**

- "Centrifugal force is the force that holds you in a roller coaster when you turn upside down. The force pushes out and not down if I spin the bucket over my head."
- "How many people have ridden an upside-down roller coaster? Raise your hands."
- "When you were upside-down did you feel like you were going to fall out?" (Answer: No)
- "Watch to see if I get wet."

Swing the bucket over your head about six times. Tell them if you slowed the bucket down, the water might fall out. The faster you spin the bucket the stronger the force will be to hold the water in the bucket.

Materials:
1. Bucket of water

* *

Group E - Student Scientific Quotes
(Omit if not using students)

Call out the names of your classroom students in Group E to come up to the microphone to do their student readings. Hand out the student copies of the readings that you are holding on the side of the center table. **See Chapter 8 - Student Scientific Quotes, page 122.** Have each student state their name and read their card. Take the cards from the students when they are finished and instruct them to be seated.

Materials:
1. Cards with student readings on them
2. Microphone

* *

* Bottle Fountain

While Group E students are reading their scientific quotes - **Have one of your students select one person from the audience.**

Bottle Fountain Materials and Directions:
1. Empty two-liter, clear, soft drink bottle
2. Modeling clay
3. Scissors
4. Drinking straw

5. Water
6. Twelve inch balloon
7. Cut a hole midway on an empty two-liter, clear, soft drink bottle.
8. Insert a drinking straw into the opening.
9. Secure the straw with modeling clay so no air can escape from the hole in the bottle.
10. Fill the bottle almost full of water. **See Diagram 19.**

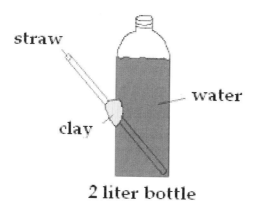

2 liter bottle

Diagram 19

11. Blow up a large balloon and with the aid of your audience helper, attach the balloon to the top of the soft drink bottle while holding the opening of the balloon closed so no air will escape. **See Diagram 20.**
12. One two-liter bottle filled with water for demonstration purposes only.

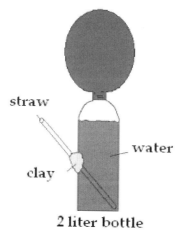

2 liter bottle

Diagram 20

Introduce your audience helper. Tell the audience that you will continue demonstrating forces in nature. Hold up the extra two-liter bottle filled with water.

Say to your volunteer:

- **"I have water in this bottle. How do you think I can get the water to come out without turning the bottle over?"**

Let the volunteer give you some suggestions for getting the water to come out of the bottle without turning it over. Take the prepared two-liter bottle from your center table. It should be almost filled up with water. ***Note** – you can only fill it as high as the top of the straw. If you fill it past the top of the straw, then the water will come out of the straw opening.

Tell the audience you will show them how to use air pressure to make the water flow out of the bottle by itself. With the volunteer holding the bottle fountain over a bucket or container to catch the water, blow up a large balloon and attach it to the top of the bottle fountain making sure you don't let go of the opening of the balloon until you are ready for the water to come out of the bottle.

Say:

- **"As soon as I let go of the balloon, the air in the balloon will push down on the water."**
- **"Since the straw is in the water, the water will come up inside of the straw and out of the top."**
- **"Everyone say the magic words, school is cool."**

When the students finish saying the magic words, release the balloon and the water will come out of the straw. Make sure your volunteer is holding the straw over a container to catch the water. See the picture below.

Have the audience give the volunteer a round of applause and instruct the volunteer to select a lollipop when he/she leaves the stage.

* *

* Rocket Launcher Have two of your students each select one person from the audience.

Introduce the volunteers to the audience. Tell the audience that you will continue demonstrating forces in nature. Explain the fact that each volunteer will take a turn and stomp on the air container. The air in the container will rush out with a great force propelling the rocket into the air. This experiment will be a contest to see which volunteer produces the most air, which will make the rocket travel the farthest.

Place the rocket launcher in front of the audience, but make sure the rocket faces away from the audience with no chance of anyone in the audience getting hurt with the flying rockets.

Have volunteer # 1 stomp on the rocket. The rocket will fly a good thirty or forty feet depending on the force of the air when it blasts off. You can count down with the audience to let the audience have a part in the experiment (e.g., 10, 9, 8, 7, 6, 5, 4, 3, 2, 1, Lift Off). Let the rocket rest at its stopping place to mark when it landed.

Have volunteer # 2 stomp on the rocket. Compare the distance between rockets. Remind the audience that air pressure moved the rockets using a natural force of nature.

Have and audience give the volunteers a round of applause for helping and have the volunteers take a lollipop on their way back to their seats.

Materials:
1. Rocket Launcher
2. Two rockets
3. Two, audience volunteers

* *

Group F - Student Scientific Quotes
(Omit if not using students)

Call out the names of your classroom students in Group F to come up to the microphone to do their student readings. Hand out the student copies of the readings that you are holding on the side of the center table. **See Chapter 8 - Student Scientific Quotes, page 122.** Have each student state their name and read their card. Take the cards from the students when they are finished and instruct them to be seated.

Materials:
1. Cards with student readings on them

2. Microphone
* *

* Balloon Race – Opposite and Equal Reaction – Have two of your students each select one person from the audience.

The directions for setting up the balloon race are in the beginning of this chapter in the section on "Stage Set Up" (page 10). **See Diagrams 1 & 2.**

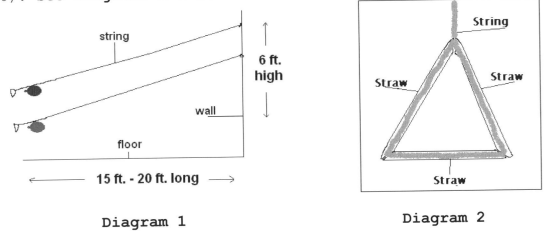

Diagram 1   Diagram 2

Tell the audience about Sir Isaac Newton's Laws of Motion.

Newton's First Law of Motion:

I. Every object in a state of uniform motion tends to remain in that state of motion unless an external force is applied to it. Newton's first law states that every object will remain at rest or in uniform motion in a straight line unless compelled to change its state by the action of an external force. This is normally taken as the definition of **inertia** (e.g., Put a chair in the middle of the stage and put a book on top of it. Tell the audience that the book will sit on the chair forever until some external or outside force moves it. Push the book off of the chair with your hand. Tell the audience that you are the larger, outside force that moved the book.).

Newton's Second Law of Motion:

II. The relationship between an object's mass m, its acceleration a, and the applied force F is $F = ma$. Acceleration and force are vectors (as indicated by their symbols being displayed in slant bold font); in this law the direction of the force vector is the same as the direction of the acceleration vector. Newton's second law of motion explains how an object will change velocity if it is pushed or pulled upon. Firstly, this law states that if you do place a force on an object, it will accelerate (e.g., change its velocity, and it will change its velocity in the direction of the force). Roll a small ball across the stage. Roll a larger ball into it, which will cause the ball to go faster in the direction of the bigger ball.

Newton's Third Law of Motion:

III. For every action there is an equal and opposite reaction.
Tell the audience you will demonstrate the 3rd Law of Motion.

Introduce your two volunteers to the audience. Give each volunteer one of the strings (that you previously set up for the balloon race experiment) to hold in their hand. Remember, they will hold the string the entire time and never let go of the string. Make sure you tell them not to let go of the string and emphasis that point. ***Note** – ask the volunteer which hand they write with and put the string in the opposite hand.

Using two different colored balloons, blow the first balloon halfway full and have one of the volunteers hold the open part of the balloon shut while you connect it to the loose piece of straw on the string, making sure none of the air escapes. One of the volunteer's hands is holding the straw handle of the string and the other hand is holding the opening of the balloon. **See Diagram 21.**

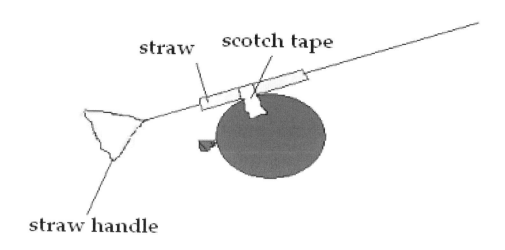

Diagram 21

Blow up the second balloon to its full capacity (much bigger then the first balloon), and have one of the volunteers hold the open part of the balloon shut while you connect it to the loose piece of straw on the string, making sure none of the air escapes. One of the volunteer's hands should be holding the straw handle of the string and the other hand should be holding the opening of the balloon. **See Diagram 22.**

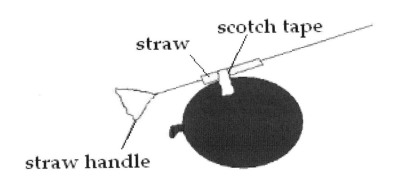

straw

scotch tape

straw handle

Diagram 22

Tell the audience that when the balloons are released, the air in the balloons will rush out of the openings in the balloons. Since the openings of the balloons are pointed towards the student, the air rushing out will push the balloons taped on the string, away from the students, demonstrating Newton's Third Law of Motion, **"For every action there is an equal and opposite reaction."**

Ask the audience which balloon will win a race when the volunteers let go of the balloons? Hold your hand over the volunteer holding the red balloon and say:

- **"How many people think red balloon will win?"**

Hold your hand over the blue balloon and say:

- **"How many people think the blue balloon will win?"**
- **"Let's count to three and then you both will let go of the balloons. 1, 2, 3."**

The smaller, red balloon will go faster, but will stop before it reaches the end of the string (make sure your string is very long). The larger balloon will make its way to the end of the string since it has more air in it. The larger, blue balloon should win the race.

After the race, go and get the balloons and take them off of the tape. Blow them up again. This time blow up the blue balloon smaller then it was before. Take the blue balloon (the smaller one) and re-attach it to the straw having the volunteer hold the opening shut so no air escapes at this time. Tape it exactly like you did the first time with the opening facing the student.

Blow up the red balloon very large, but this time when you tape it to the straw on the string, turn the opening of the balloon to the side and not to the back of the string facing the student. **See Diagram 23.**

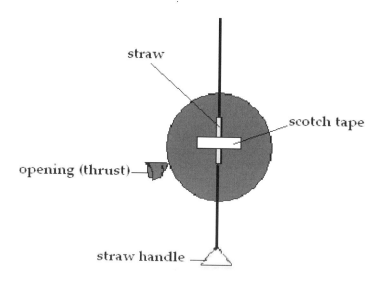

straw

scotch tape

opening (thrust)

straw handle

Diagram 23

Having the opening off to the side of the balloon will change the direction of the trust of the balloon. The air coming out of the balloon will come out to the side and push the balloon in the opposite direction, but the balloon is taped to the straw on the string, which is facing opposite of the student. Instead of going straight ahead on the string, the balloon will spin around on the string.

When you are set up and ready to go, or while you are talking to the audience and blowing up the balloons say:

- **"I want to tell you about variables."**
- **"Variables are something in an experiment that will make a change."**
- **"Everyone say, variable."**
- **"I have introduced a variable in this experiment."**

Again ask the audience which balloon will win the race when the volunteers let go of the balloons? Hold your hand over the volunteer holding the red balloon and say:

- **"How many people think red balloon will win?"**

Hold your hand over the blue balloon and say:

- **"How many people think the blue balloon will win?"**

From the last race, the students will now know that the larger balloon should win the race and will yell louder for the larger balloon. The smaller balloon will win the race, since the larger balloon will travel a short distance and just spin around the string. This should surprise the audience.

Say:
- **"Let's count to three and then you both will let go of the balloons. 1, 2, 3."**

After the race when the audience stops laughing, explain what you did to create a variable. Explain that Newton's 3rd Law of Motion says for every reaction, there is an opposite and equal reaction. The air in the balloon was coming out of the balloon, which was taped on the string sideways so the balloon tried to go sideways, but it was tapped to the straw on the string which was going straight, so that made the balloon spin.

Have the audience give the volunteers a round of applause and instruct the volunteers to select a lollipop when they leave the stage.

Materials:
1. Large balloons (at least 6 incase of breakage)
2. Ball of string
4. Plastic straws (at least 4)
5. Scotch tape
6. Scissors
* *

Group G - Student Scientific Quotes
(Omit if not using students)

Call out the names of your classroom students in Group G to come up to the microphone to do their student readings. Hand out the student copies of the readings that you are holding on the side of the center table. **See Chapter 8 - Student Scientific Quotes, page 122.** Have each student state their name and read their card. Take the cards from the students when they are finished and instruct them to be seated.

Materials:
1. Cards with student readings on them
2. Microphone

* *

* Forces - Crushing Egg in Hand - Have six of your students select two people each from the audience.

Continuing with forces, introduce your volunteers from the audience and have them spread out across the stage so everyone can see them. ***Note** - Have your students pick some adults and large men from the audience to show that even strong adults can't do this next experiment.

Tell the audience that you will show them another experiment using a force in nature.

Give each person a large, plastic bag (zip lock bags are great). Explain to the audience that you will give each of the volunteers a raw egg, and you want them to squeeze the egg until it breaks. You might want to break an egg in front of the audience to show them how easily the eggs will break.

Say:

- "When the volunteers squeeze the egg, the force they create will just go around and around on the egg, and it won't break."
- "You can make a lot of money on this experiment."
- "Go home and tell your dad or mom that you bet them five dollars that they can't break a raw egg by squeezing it."

As you are talking, demonstrate the procedure to the audience and say:

- "Let me show you how to do it."
- "First, make sure you don't have any rings on your fingers."

- "Open up your palm and place the egg in the center of your palm."
- "Gently roll your fingers around the egg."
- "Hold your thumb out and do not use your thumb to squeeze the egg."
- "Do not poke your fingers into the egg or move your fingers from around the egg."

Go up to each volunteer and make sure they are not wearing a ring. Have them open their palms with their thumb extended out and place an egg in their hand and roll their finger around the egg. Have them place their hands inside of the plastic bag before they squeeze incase of any accidents. Sometimes the egg will break if there is a small crack in the egg.

Say:
- "We will all count to three and then I want everyone to squeeze your egg as hard as you can to see if you can break it."
- "1, 2, 3, squeeze."

The volunteers should not be able to break the eggs. However, there will always be someone who cheats or has a crack in their egg, so be prepared for it.

Let them squeeze for a minute and then take the eggs and plastic bags away from the volunteers. Have the audience give them a round of applause and have the volunteers take a lollipop before they leave the stage.

Materials:
1. One, dozen eggs (as many as you purchase)
2. One, dozen large, plastic bags (zip lock are the best)
****

* Hoberman Sphere – Expanding/Contracting – Have three of your students select one person each from the audience.

How many Hoberman spheres you purchase, will be the factor on how many students you bring up on stage. ***Note** – One sphere is sufficient for the experiment, but I got a great deal on the spheres and purchased five of them.

Introduce two new vocabulary words to the audience, **expanding** and **contracting (expand or contract)**.

Say:
- "Remember earlier in the show when we talked about matter and atoms?"

- "Well in nature, when matter gets hot it expands or gets larger."
- "When it gets cold, it contracts or gets smaller or goes back to its original size."

Hold up one of the Hoberman spheres and demonstrate expanding and contracting to the audience while you are talking to the audience.

Say:
- "This is called a Hoberman Sphere."
- "The sphere is made up of six intersecting circles with 20 triangles and 12 pentagons."
- "How many sides does a triangle have?" (Answer: 3)
- "How many sides does a pentagon have?" (Answer: 5)
- "In an explosion, energy expands outward in straight lines from the center in all directions."
- "This sphere is like an explosion since it opens in all directions at the same time."

Open and close the Hoberman sphere for the audience. When you open it, say the word, **expanding**, or getting bigger. When you close the sphere, say the word, **contracting**, or getting smaller.

Explain that when air molecules get hot they expand (open the sphere) and when air molecules get cold they contract (close the sphere).

Give your volunteer(s) a sphere and have them open or close the sphere as you say the words, **expand and contract.** Try to trick them and say, expand, expand, contract, expand, contract, contract...to see what they will do.

Have your volunteer(s) hold the sphere by opposite sides and throw the sphere up in the air. As they throw the sphere, have them pull the sphere open. As they catch the sphere, have them shut it. **See Diagram 24.**

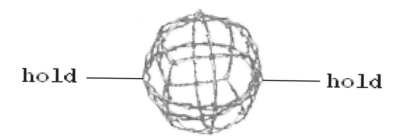

hold ———— ———— hold

Diagram 24

Have the audience give the volunteer(s) a round of applause and instruct the volunteer(s) to select a lollipop when he/she leaves the stage.

Materials:
1. Hoberman Sphere(s) (as many as you purchase)
****

* Crushing Cans - with Air Pressure

Hold up an empty soda can (Coke, Sprite, any aluminum can will do), and tell them that you will crush the can using air pressure. Tell the audience that the can is empty and turn the can upside down to show them that it is empty.

Say:
- **"The can doesn't have any liquid in it, but is it really empty?"** (Answer: No, it is filled with air.)
- **"It is filled with air."**
- **"If I were to heat the air in this can, will the molecules of air expand or contract?"** (Answer: expand)
- **"The molecules will expand and stretch out and fill the can with big air molecules."**

Demonstrate as you are talking and say:

- **"I am going to put two spoons of water into the can and hold it over my gas stove."**

Light the gas stove and hold the can using long tongs to protect your hands from the fire.

Say:
- **"In nature there are three states of matter, solid, liquid and gas."**
- **"Water in its natural state is a liquid."**
- **"When water freezes it becomes a...?"** (Answer: solid)
- **"When water gets hot and boils, it becomes a...?"** (Answer: gas)
- **"I am going to heat the water and the liquid will turn into a gas and make steam."**
- **"When we see a nice stream of steam coming out of the can we will know that the air inside of the can is expanded and very hot."**
- **"When we are ready, I will say, 1, 2, 3, and I will turn the can upside down into the cold water."**

- "The air in the can will shrink or contract extremely fast and will make a loud boom and crush the can."
- "It will also create a vacuum and will suck water into the can to fill the place of the missing air molecules."
- "We are ready, say, 1, 2, 3."

When the steam is really coming out of the can, quickly turn the can upside down into the bowl of water. The can will crush and make a loud boom.

The audience will love the loud sound. Hold the can up over the bowl above the water and show them the water the vacuum caused to be sucked up into the can. There will be a good amount of water spilling out of the can at this point.

Do the experiment again as the students will want to watch more closely so see if you crushed the can with your tongs.

Materials:
1. Small, propane, gas stove
2. Water
3. Spoon
4. Bowl filled with water
5. Large tongs
6. Empty, aluminum cans
7. Paper towels or rags to wipe up any spills

* *

* Alcohol/Water…Fire Experiment

Say:

- "I'm going to show you an experiment that is very dangerous. Again, I need you to hold up your right hand and repeat after me."

*Note – Turn your back to the audience and hold up your right hand to show the smaller students the correct hand to hold up.

Say:

- "I promise,"
- "I will not try this experiment at home."

Tell the audience you have special chemicals and supplies that they don't have, so they can't do the experiment and they might get hurt if they play with fire at home.

Explain what you are doing to the audience as you are doing the experiment.

Say:

- "**Look at this white handkerchief.**" (Open it up and show it to the audience and wave it around to show them that there are no marks on it.)
- "**I have two special chemicals here on the table.**"
- "**I will dip the handkerchief into chemical #1 and squeeze out any excess chemical.**" (Dip the handkerchief into a glass half-filled with water to protect the fibers of the cloth and squeeze out the excess.)
- "**I will now dip the handkerchief into chemical #2 and squeeze out any excess chemical.**" (Dip it into the glass half-filled with alcohol and squeeze out the excess.)
- "**Using these very long tongs, I will light the handkerchief.**" (Grasp the handkerchief with very long tongs and light the handkerchief.)

The fire will make a huge blue/yellow flame. Holding the handkerchief over your bowl of water (incase you need to put out the fire quickly) let it burn for about five to six seconds (just enough time for the audience to see a huge flame). Put the handkerchief into the bowl of water. Sometimes the fire might continue to burn on top of the bowl of water. That will amaze the students since they all know that water puts out fires.

*Note – Make sure that you don't knock over your glass half-filled with alcohol while you are burning the handkerchief. Place the glass of alcohol away from your experiment.

Do the experiment again if you want to amaze the students one more time.

When you are finished, unfold the handkerchief and hold it up in front of the audience and say:

- **"Everyone saw the fire. Where is the carbon?"**
- **"The handkerchief is not burned or discolored."**

The handkerchief should be nice and white. ***Note** – Be carefull not to let the handkerchief burn for more then six seconds as it will burn and discolor.

Ask the audience to think why the handkerchief didn't burn and to discuss it with their teachers when they return to class.

<u>Materials</u>:
1. Clear glass half full of water
2. Clear glass half full of rubbing alcohol
3. Large tongs
4. Lighter or matches
5. Large bowl filled with water
6. White handkerchief
7. Cigarette lighter or matches
8. Paper towels or rags to wipe up any spills

* *

* Van de Graaf Generator…Static Electricity – Hair Raising

Saving the best for last, tell the audience that you will make lightning on stage using atoms. It would be best if the lights in the room were dimmed for the next experiment.

Again, explain to the audience what you are doing as you get ready for the experiment. Put on a pair of black, insulated rubber gloves to protect yourself from small shocks from the generator. Hold up a small fluorescent light bulb and wrap the bottom with a kitchen dishtowel (this will usually save you from the shock). ***Note** – using a small power strip with an "on" and "off" button works the best. Plug the generator into the power strip and turn the switch on. The Van de Graaf Generator will start to hum separating the positive and negative electrons in the air. The positive electrons are collected in the small silver dome of the generator.

Say:

- **"If I hold this fluorescent light bulb close to the top of the generator, the protons will arc out and light up the light bulb."**

Hold the light bulb close to the dome of the generator and the electricity will arc over to the bulb, ignite the gas in the bulb and make it light up for a second. ***Note** - The last time I did this experiment, I made the room as dark as possible. I gave a camera with no film in it to another teacher and told her to use the flash and take a pretend picture of me holding the bulb close to the generator when the bulb lit up. Every time she snapped a picture and the flash went off, the audience thought the generator made lightning and the students screamed. The bulb would light up; the camera would flash; and the students would scream. What an awesome trick to play on the audience.

When you are finished with the light bulb and have turned the generator off, touch the dome of the generator with a metal spoon to take the remaining shock out of the dome. Otherwise, if you touch the dome you will get a minor shock.

Use yourself as a volunteer. Take off all of the jewelry on your hands and stand on a plastic container to get your feet off of the ground. Place one of your hands on the dome of the generator and have someone else turn it on using the power button on the power switch. Make sure you don't touch anything else while you are connected to the generator. Directions will come with the generator.

I had all the students raise their right hands and promise not to laugh when I did this next experiment.

You will begin to feel all of the hair on your body stand on end. The hair on your head will slowly rise up in the air and try to get away from each other. (The longer and thinner your hair, the better for the audience.) ***Note** - Since I have light colored hair, I had two, parent volunteers stand behind me holding a black piece of cardboard to give contrast to my hair so the audience could see my hair better. The only problem, they accidentally hit my head with the cardboard, and I got a little shock when the cardboard touched my hair.

You can call as many students up on the stage to try this experiment as you like, but emphasize the point that they can not lift their hand from the generator as long as it is turned on, or they will be shocked. Have someone at the power switch at all times ready to turn the generator off when the volunteer calls it quits. Again, when the generator is turned off, the person will have a slight shock in their body. You can touch the dome of the generator with a metal spoon after the generator has been turned off and before the volunteer lifts their hand, or the fun thing for my students was to have the volunteer go out and touch someone in the audience and pass the small shock to them.

Materials:
1. Van de Graaf Generator
2. Black, insulated, rubber gloves
3. Dish towel
4. Large, plastic, milk crate
5. Power strip with on/off switch
6. Fluorescent, light bulb
7. Large spoon or metal object

* *

* <u>End of show without classroom students</u>:

If you are not using your classroom students in the presentation, this is the end of the show. Thank the audience for their participation and good behavior. Ask them to draw a picture of their favorite part of the show, or write a paragraph telling you what they liked about the show, what they would like to see more of, or just any comments they would like to share with you about the presentation.

Play the "Star Wars" sound track as the students leave the room. Be creative and make your own ending for the show.

If you are using your classroom students in the production please go to the next ending – "Mission Control" song.

* *

* Mission Control Song

Have the Commander say:

- **"Attention."**

The students will rise and stand at attention. The Commander will say:

- **"Line up."**

The students will line up across the stage. Once the students are in position and ready for the song, the commander will say:

- **"At ease."**

The students will stand with their hands behind their backs (most of them will forget and put their hands down at their side). Turn on the tape of the song "Mission Control" (if you were able to find the cassette), or have someone play the piano while your class sings the song. **See Chapter 13 – Music, page 151.**

Have your students do any hand movements while they are singing the song (e.g., point up to the sky when they mention Mars). Have your students salute the audience and bow when the song is finished.

Materials:
1. Piano or cassette/CD player
2. Sheet Music
3. Microphone
4. Optional – Cassette of "Mission Control" song

* <u>End of show with classroom students</u>:

If you are using your classroom students in the presentation, this is the end of the show. Thank the audience for their participation and good behavior. Ask them to draw a picture of their favorite part of the show, or write a paragraph telling you what they liked about the show, what they would like to see more of, or just any comments they would like to share with you about the presentation.

Play the "Star Wars" sound track as the students leave the room. Be creative and make your own ending for the show.

MY BEST WISHES FOR A GREAT PERFORMANCE!

Chapter 3

Program

Please see **Appendix A** for a sample of a program you can create to pass out to parents, teachers and visitors who come to the presentation. The parents can use the program to help remember the simple science experiments used in the presentation so they can try them at home with their child. ***Note** - Make a double-sided copy and fold in the center.

Space, Science & Other Things

Name of School
Principal: Name
Assistant Principal: Name
Your Name: Grade Room

Date   Time

Outside of the program

Picture of your class

Special Thank you

Principal…………………………Name

Assistant Principal……………Name

Parents & Volunteers…………Names

Any one else you want to thank.

Space, Science & Other Things

Name of School
Principal: Name
Assistant Principal: Name
Your Name: Grade Room

Date   Time

Inside of the program

Program
* Introduction… "Landing of the Endeavor" … all students
* Science is Magic… magic tricks
* "I've Got the Power"… **4** audience dancers
* Knowledge is Power… ping pong balls… student names
* Chemical/Physical Changes… magic paper
* Mission: To get students excited about Science and the Science Fair
* Surprise Visitors… student names

SIMPLE SCIENCE EXPERIMENTS
* Matter… Balloons
* Balloon pop with pin… **1** audience helper
* Acids/Bases… vinegar & baking soda gases
  * Volcano in a glass
  * Blow balloon up with baking soda/vinegar
  * Blow cork off bottle with baking soda/vinegar
* Surprise Visitors
* Air Bags… Air Pressure… **12** audience helpers
* Sound Vibrations… Chicken Cups… **12** audience helpers
* Shuttle Telephone… **2** audience helpers
* Surprise Visitors
* Forces:
  * Centrifugal Force… bucket of water
  * Bottle Fountain… **1** audience helper
  * Rocket Launcher… **2** audience helpers
  * Balloon Race… **2** audience helpers
  * Crushing Egg in Hand… **12** audience helpers
* Hoberman Sphere – Expanding & Contracting… **3** audience helpers

* Crushing Cans with Air Pressure… teacher
* Fire – Handkerchief Experiment… teacher
* Van de Graaf Generator… static electricity, hair raising

FINALE – *MISSION CONTROL*

CAST

CAPCOM………………………STUDENT NAME
FLIGHT DIRECTOR……………STUDENT NAME
MEDICAL OFFICER……………STUDENT NAME
WEATHER PLANE………………STUDENT NAME
COMMANDER……………………STUDENT NAME
NAVIGATION……………………STUDENT NAME
LAB #1…………………………STUDENT NAME
PAO #1…………………………STUDENT NAME
PAO #2…………………………STUDENT NAME
PILOT…………………………STUDENT NAME
CREW #1………………………STUDENT NAME
CREW #2………………………STUDENT NAME
CREW #3………………………STUDENT NAME
CREW #4………………………STUDENT NAME
CREW #5………………………STUDENT NAME
CREW #6………………………STUDENT NAME
CREW #7………………………STUDENT NAME
DIRECTOR/TEACHER…………YOUR NAME

Thank you for coming to our performance. See you in space!

"Over and out!"

Chapter 4

Magic Tricks

To get the audience's attention very quickly, always start the show with magic. Everyone loves magic and it's great to see the smiles of amazement on the children's faces. Tell the audience that **"science is magic, or is it?"**

Below is a web site for a great online magic shop for you to purchase all of the materials for the tricks used in the show. How much magic you want to do in your presentation depends on how much you want to spend. Research **www.google.com** to find other online shops where you might find the same products at a cheaper price, although the prices are fairly consistent, considering what they cost six years ago.

Use the chapter titled *Teacher's Guide* for the "when, where, and what" to say for each trick. You don't have to follow the dialogue exactly, but it's there to give you an idea as to how to use the tricks. More important, be creative!

Trick # 1 - **Floating Ball Trick** - $7.95
http://www.magictricks.com/closeup/invsreel.htm

* Web site description - "Use this gimmick to make a ball, dollar bill or other light object float in midair! You can do this anywhere! This is the economy version of this amazing floating gimmick. The clear, plastic cylinder contains about 6 feet of microfine thread on a reel, and has a small pin to attach it to the underside of a collar, the inside of a shirt, etc. Thread can be extended about three feet, can be anchored on an object with the piece of wax that is included, and retracts back into the cylinder when released. When the thread breaks, more thread can be fed from inside the cylinder. Thread and mechanism are delicate; careful handling required (this is very, very fine thread - that's what makes it "invisible"). The thread does not break after every use; with careful handling, you can get many uses out of the length of thread that comes in this reel. Refills are actually more expensive than the cost of a new reel, so we don't carry them. When the reel is empty, just purchase another one - it's cheaper than buying a refill!"

Use this trick to start the show by making a small ball appear to float in midair. This really gets everyone's attention. Use a ball that is in two pieces like the plastic Easter eggs you can fill with candy. Using a bit of tacky wax, the kind that you stick papers onto walls and bulletin boards, stick some wax on the inside of the ball, attach the micro fiber, and close the ball. You can find a small LCD light and a watch battery and make the ball light up allowing the audience to see it better. Run the micro fiber over the top of your head, behind your head and down your arm and attach the other end of the micro fiber to a ring using the tacky wax again. When you lift your arm, the ball goes down. When you move your head, the ball follows the direction of your head. When you lower your arm, the ball goes up. The micro fiber is black and so small that the audience can't see it. You can really make any small item seem to float. The students will be amazed. The audience will be able to see the fiber if you are too close to them and there is a lot of sunlight, so avoid getting too close.

Trick # 2 - Small LOTA BOWL - $29.00

* **Web site description** - "Great prop. Pour a quantity of water from the bowl, seeming to empty it. A few minutes later, again pour a quantity of water from the container, apparently emptying it. But no! A few minutes later, you again pour water from the bowl. Endless possibilities."

Fill the small bowl with water and set it on the side of the stage. During various parts of the show, stop what you are doing and look over at the vase sitting on the stage. Slowly walk over to it and carry it over to a bucket you have placed on the stage. Dump out the water and re-place it to its original spot on the stage. Continue to empty the vase during various parts of the show. About the third time you dump it out the audience will start to laugh and wonder where the extra water came from in the vase. You can dump water out of the vase about ten or twelve times before it's finally empty. Great gag.

Trick # 3 - STANDARD THUMB TIP - Disappearing Hanky - $3.95

* Web site description - "The one "must have" gimmick for every magician! Probably the most popular and most used device in magic, this utility device makes it possible to vanish silks, cigarettes, salt- even water- in your bare hand. You can use it to produce items as well! Keep one of these in every pocket- you'll use it often."

9-INCH SILK - $1.95 to be used with the above thumb.

Produce a silk handkerchief from thin air! Red is a great color.

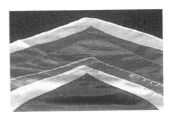

* Web site description - "The one "must have" gimmick for every magician! Probably the most popular and most used device in magic, this utility device makes it possible to vanish silks, cigarettes, salt- even water- in your bare hand. You can use it to produce items as well! Keep one of these in every pocket- you'll use it often!"

While you wave a red hanky in front of the audience, tell them that you will make it disappear. The placement of the thumb on your hand depends if you are right or left-handed. If you are right-handed, then place the thumb on your right hand. If you are left-handed, then place the thumb on your left hand.

Say you are right-handed. Put the fake thumb on your right thumb. Hold the hanky over the fake thumb. Show the audience that you have nothing in your left hand. Switch the hanky to your left hand and show the audience that you don't have anything in your right hand. Be sure to point your fingers out to the audience so they don't notice that your right thumb is just a bit longer then it should be.

When you transfer the hanky back to your right hand, secretly take off the thumb and slip it into the palm of your left hand. With your left palm closed over the fake thumb, begin to stuff the hanky into the hollow of the thumb. For the last stuff, push your right thumb into the fake thumb. Hold it there, and ask the audience to say the magic words, **school is cool**. When you pull your hands apart and hold them up to the audience, the red hanky has disappeared. The audience will yell and be amazed. You can then decide if you have ended the trick, or you can make the hanky reappear by taking the fake thumb back in your left hand and slowly pull out the hanky from your left palm. The last pull, make sure you slip the thumb back onto your right hand. Ask the audience to think about how you did the trick.

Trick # 4 - DOUBLE ZIPPER CHANGE BAG - $35.00

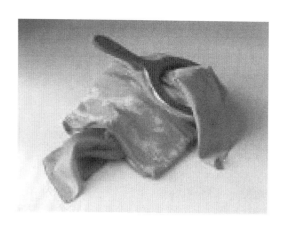 

* **Web site description** - "Place an item in the bag. Instantly turn the bag inside out to show that the item has vanished! The item can be made to reappear if desired. Also can be used to exchange one item for another. Show the bag empty; put a blue silk into it. Reach in- the blue silk has now become a red one! Great for doing a blendo routine, mismade flag, etc. Double bag with zipper at the bottom so you can push your hand right through to show the bag "empty", or just use as an ordinary change bag."

Use a small toy for this trick. Small, squeaky stuffed animals work the best. Hold up the toy to the audience and make it squeak making the students laugh. Tell them that you are going to make the toy disappear. Turn the magic bag upside down and show them that it's empty. Turn the bag inside out to show them that it's empty. Return the bag to its original position and drop the toy into the magic bag. Have the audience say the magic words, **school is cool,** and while they are yelling at you, push the switch on the bag and the bag will move to its hidden secret compartment. Turn the bag over and the mouse will not fall out. Push the bag inside out and the audience will see that the toy is gone. Have the audience say the magic words again, and push the switch and turn the bag over and the mouse will fall out. You can select a small student from the audience to help you with the trick. Have the student drop the mouse inside of the bag and look inside of it to verify to the audience that it has disappeared.

Trick # 5 - COLOR CHANGING HANKY - $8.95

* **Web site description** - "A blue and a green handkerchief are tied together. When the performer pulls the hanks through his hand, they magically change to a red and a yellow handkerchief! When he pulls them through his hand again, they change back to a blue and a green handkerchief. Can be repeated over and over instantly!"

Please follow the very easy directions enclosed with the handkerchiefs.

Trick # 6 – Card in Orange trick

You will need two decks of identical playing cards. **Before the show starts** pick out a card from one deck, like the Ace of Hearts and discard the rest of that deck. Fold the card into fourths and cut out one of the sections and save it for later use. See diagram.

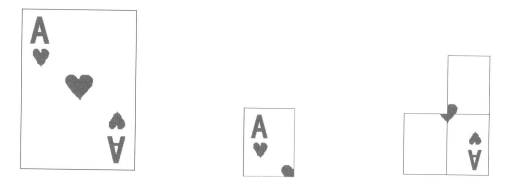

Fold the remaining card (with the section missing out of it) and make a small cut in the bottom of an orange. Slide the folded card into the orange and place it by the Mission Control board on a paper towel and never go near the orange during the first part of the show.

Tell the audience that there is so much power and knowledge in the room and we all know that knowledge is power. Tell them that we are going to use the power of **"telekinesis"** to make a card disappear and reappear inside the orange across the room.

Select a volunteer from the audience (chose a very small child who won't be able to see you fix the deck). While you are waiting for the volunteer to come up on stage, take the disappearing magic bag from the table and secretly put the ¼ section of the card (that you stored on the center table) into one section of the magic bag and flip the switch.

Holding a new deck of cards in your hands with your back slightly to audience, tell the child to tell you when to stop shuffling the cards. Always have the Ace of Hearts on the bottom of the deck with your finger on it to protect it from being shuffled. When the child tells you to stop, turn the deck over and give the Ace of Hearts to the child. Have the child hold it up to the audience.

Say:
- **"So your card is the Ace of Hearts."**

Have the child fold the card in half and then fold it in half again which makes fourths. Then, have the child tear the card in half and then into fourths. Show the audience that the bag is empty and have the child look into the bag to verify that it's empty. Have the child drop all four pieces of the card into the disappearing bag. Flip the switch. Then have the students say the magic words, **school is cool,** and when you turn the bag over, only one piece of the card will fall out (the piece you cut out from the first deck of cards).

Pretend to look shocked and puzzled. Walk over to the orange and using a sharp knife, cut the orange from the top very carefully. Smile and pull out the hidden card in the orange. When you open the card, one of the sections will naturally be missing. Then walk over to the stage, pick up the missing piece of card that fell out of your magic bag. Tell the audience that the trick almost worked but you think some of the audience needs to stay in school to get more knowledge. It's an amazing trick. Good luck.

*Note - the longer you keep the card in the orange, the more it will be wet. Put some plastic wrap around the card in the orange to keep it dry. You can easily cut the plastic wrap away with a knife.

OTHER MATERIALS: USED IN SHOW

Use the chapter titled *Teacher's Guide* for usage.

* <u>D'Lite Magic Thumb Tip</u> - $19.75 a pair

http://www.hobbytron.net/D'Lite-Soft-Tip-Pair.html?AID=10289
758&PID=1014613

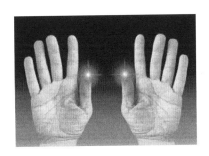

* Web site description - "The thumb tips allow you to summon a bright red light to your fingertips on command, the D'Lite pair lets you create the same enchanting effect, but with two sparks of light instead of one! Toss them from hand to hand, hide them in a bag, find them playing behind the ear of a spectator! Say that they're fairies or fire or stars plucked from the sky - whatever you decide, you'll enchant and delight with this fabulous trick."

* <u>Magic Flash Paper</u>

FLASH PAPER (4)	ITEM # BUC04	PRICE $7.50
FLASH PAPER (100)	ITEM # BUC08	PRICE $150.00

http://www.daytonamagic.com/Fire%20Magic/F01.htm

* **Web site description** – "Flash items are used for dove pans, flames from the air, flash pots, and fire effects of many kinds. Anyone who has seen a magician use flash paper knows that it adds that little "extra" to the performance.

SAFETY NOTE - We at Daytona Magic emphasize to all prospective purchasers that **FIRE TRICKS AND FLASH PRODUCTS** are **NOT FOR CHILDREN! We do not knowingly sell flash or fire items to children. We recommend these items only to be used by professional magicians. We have no control once the item leaves our premises. Therefore we accept no responsibility for their use or misuse.**"

Another web site with reasonable prices:

http://www.magical-tricks.com/FireMagic2.htm

Flash Paper

2x3 inch 20 sheets   - $7.99   8x9 inch 4 sheets - $10.99

* **Web site description** – "This is Magician's Flash Paper. Produce flames from your fingertips. Paper ignites into brilliant flame when touched by a lighter or match. Can be used for dozens of effects. It contains 20 sheets. Can be cut or torn into many smaller pieces. For use by professionals at their own risk. Buyer must be 18+ There are other interesting products on this site that you can use for your show."

* <u>Knowledge is Power</u> – Open & Closed Circuits

<u>http://www.schoolmasters.com/search.html</u>

The above web site is where I purchased the remaining supplies for the show. You can phone 1-800-654-4321 for a free catalog.

Metal Strips

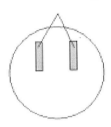

* <u>Glow Ball</u> – $3.95

* **Web site description** – "By touching two metal strips simultaneously your body becomes a path for charged molecules to complete a circuit. Result-the ball glows brightly. Works with several people creating the path. When opened, the energy ball reveals a working circuit for insight into the world of computers."

* <u>Van de Graaf Generator</u> – $159.95 assembled
$129.95 Unassembled

* **Web site description** – Demonstrator of static electricity. In use for over 25 years. Consists of aluminum collector sphere mounted above neoprene belt; sturdy base and removable terminal housing for easy viewing of working parts; one each, metal and plastic pulley to generate different electrical charges. Uses include: demonstration of high voltage phenomena, demonstration of electrostatic attraction and repulsion, as a substitute for the

Wimshurst generator, and experiments with hair raising, lightning, and electric wind. Assembled weight 2.3 kg, kit weight 2.1 kg. 200,000-volt potential, operable in humidities up to 90%. 45 cm high, 19 cm diam. aluminum collector sphere. Uses 110 volt 60 cycle AC. Includes spare neoprene belt. 1/150 hp motor. Convenient tabletop size. Full range of replacement parts available."

* <u>Windbags</u> – $5.95 /Pkg of 4

Eight-foot long plastic bags for experiments with air pressure

* <u>Stomp Rocket Launcher</u> – $14.95 Each

http://www.sciencekit.com

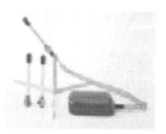

* **Web site description** – "Comprises rocket launcher and re-useable air powered rockets, jump on the 'Stomp Pad' and propel your rocket up to 400ft into the air! They need no batteries or fuel and are great fun in the park or on the beach. Supplied complete with Stomp Pad and Hose, Stand and 3 High Performance Rockets."

* Hoberman Sphere - $24.00

http://www.school-tech.com/physsci.html

http://www.hobermansphere.com

http://www.discian.com/resources/tools/hoberman_home.htm

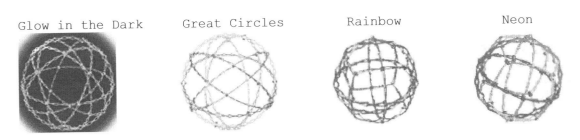

Glow in the Dark   Great Circles   Rainbow   Neon

* **Web site description** - "The Hoberman Sphere is a mechanical structure made of slightly curved links (or struts) joined by pivots into "scissor-pairs". These basic components are connected by hubs into larger units. The opening and closing of the scissor-pairs results in the folding and unfolding, expansion and contraction motion of the sphere. If you look around, you will find other structures that use similar linkage systems for example, folding gates and clothes-drying racks. The Hoberman Sphere is a type of spherical polyhedron (a multi-sided solid geometric form) known as an icosadodecahedron. If you know Greek, the name tells you exactly what it is: a geometric form (-hedron) combining 20 (I osa-) and 12 (dodeca) 20 triangles and 12 pentagons. The Hoberman Sphere is made up of six intersecting circles. Because it is a closed unit, a circle is stronger than a straight line; in addition, each point of intersection reinforces the stru6ture, making it even stronger. The Hoberman Sphere always maintains this strength, because its shape never changes as it expands and contracts. The shape remains the same because the Sphere is a precise geometric mechanism where art meets engineering. Some people have said the expanding Sphere looks like a fireworks display. In an explosion, energy expands outward in straight lines from the center in all directions. The Hoberman Sphere expands in the same way: as it opens and closes, the hubs ride along invisible straight lines that intersect its center. Other people have compared the Sphere's motion to the opening of a flower and the shape to forms in nature like the skeleton of a radiolarian (a tiny sea animal) which consists of struts joined into a sphere. Call (888) 229-3653 for more information about the Hoberman Retailer nearest you."

21 Things You Can Do with the Hoberman Sphere

From the Discian Group web site:

http://www.discian.com/resources/tools/hoberman_home.htm

1 - Balancing act. Open the sphere and balance it on one hand. See how long you can balance it there without it closing or flipping over.

2 - Flip down. Hold the closed sphere by one hub on top of your open palm. Flip the sphere over and watch it open. Then flip it back to the top of your palm and let it close. When you've gotten good at this, try it with your other hand!

3 - Open bounce. A rug works best for this. Open the sphere fully. Holding the sphere open with two hands, toss it down to the floor. If you spin it toward you, it will bounce back into your hands. Do not try to bounce the sphere when it is closed!

4 - Toss-up. Throw the sphere up above your head as you pull out on opposite hubs. It will open as it goes up and close as it comes down. Catch it!

5 - Two-person catch. Throw the sphere to another person. If you spin the sphere slightly as you throw, it will open in mid-air. (Let your partner know it's coming before you throw it!)

6 - Open spin. A hard floor works best for this. Open the sphere and place it on the floor. Holding an upper hub, spin the sphere and watch it move. Try spinning it on a hub, then a triangle, then a pentagon notice the different way it moves on each of these shapes.

7 - Ballerina spin. Hold the open sphere by its top hub, with the bottom hub on the ground. Spin it around by the hub as you spin around it. See how long you can keep it open. If you get dizzy, spin the other way!

8 - Square dance spin. Keep the open sphere spinning as above. Start with the sphere in front of you and your right hand on the hub, continue to face in the same direction as you spin the hub behind you and switch to your left hand. You spin around the sphere as the sphere spins around you!

9 - Two-handed spin. With the sphere in closed position, place your hands on either side. Grasp a hub on each side and spin the sphere. Pull out on the hubs to twirl it open.

10 - Mid-air bounce. Hold the nearly open sphere balanced with the bottom hub on top of your open hand. Steady it with your other hand either at the top or side. Now quickly push the bottom hub up to close the sphere as you let go with the steadying hand. It will appear to bounce closed and then open again in the air. Catch it before it drops! Repeat. (This one takes a little practice.)

11 - Mid-air bounce and spin. Do the same as above, but spin the sphere as you push up on the bottom hub.

12 - Two-handed spin open-to-close. Hold opposite hubs on the open sphere between your thumb and first two fingers. Spin and twirl the sphere as you close it. Now try the reverse. (This takes practice, but looks really cool!)

13 - Continuous roll. Open the sphere and roll it in front of you across the floor. Watch it close. If you have a large open space, you can run behind it and continue to roll it, keeping it open by hitting the underpart of the upper hub. Races, anyone?

14 - Mesmerizing. Holding the sphere by opposite hubs with your hands on either side, open and close the sphere as fast as you can, staring at the center.

15 - Spikey hat. Wear the Hoberman Sphere on top of your head, opening it just enough to fit and stay on. Turn this into a cool activity by balancing it on your head as you walk, run, dance or move creatively. Try this in public! Also good for relay races.

16 - Space helmet. Open the sphere enough to fit your whole head inside it, then close it to fit comfortably and let it rest on your shoulders. (We don't recommend running while wearing the Hoberman Sphere helmet!)

17 - Thinking cap. An artist we know puts the sphere over his head when he is trying to think of a new idea. and expands it when the idea comes to him.

18 - Sphereman. If you are small enough, you can wear the sphere around your middle.

19 - Gimme Shelter. If you are small enough, place the sphere pentagon side down on a rug and climb inside. Have a seat!

20 - Double fun. If you have two spheres, put on sphere closed on the ground. Now place a pentagon of the second sphere over it in opened position. Reach in and open the inner sphere. Lift them up and drop them. Watch them close together. What would happen with three spheres?

21 - Mobile. Hang it from the ceiling to make a room decoration that you can open & close. Follow directions in booklet enclosed in the box with your sphere.

Grown-ups: Many of these activities are fun for grown-ups, too. Try incorporating them into your exercise routine for a fun upper-body workout! Parents: Besides being fun, perfecting these activities require a child (or grown-up) to practice physical and hand-eye coordination. Playing with the Hoberman Sphere is a fun way to exercise both your body and your creativity. We recommend most of these activities for school-age and up, some of them may be unsuitable for younger children.

©1999, All Rights Reserved, Kevin Eikenberry. Kevin is the President of The Kevin Eikenberry Group, a learning consulting company that helps their Clients reach their potential through a variety of training, consulting and speaking services. Go to **http://www.kevineikenberry.com/training/training.asp** to learn more about our customized training services offered or contact Kevin at toll free 888.LEARNER/**Kevin@KevinEikenberry.com.**

* <u>Mission Communicators</u> - $29.95

http://www.farmgoodsforkids.com/um-5005.html

* Web site description – "This set of two long-range walkie-talkie communicators is designed with dual-channel circuitry to allow you to talk and listen without pushing a button. Each communicator features a headset and multi-function wrist unit with built-in LCD clock, compass and removable magnifier. Up to 600 foot range! Requires (2) two 9-volt batteries (Not Included). CM5 Headset Features: adjustable headband; built-in earphone and microphone;

range of up to 600 feet (180 meters) at line of sight; flexible antenna."

Great site to get more ideas for the show

Photo taken from an image in the Kodak electronic photo gallery.

Jeff Lindsay's Magic Page

 http://www.jefflindsay.com/magic.html#myshow

Chapter 5

Building the Space Shuttle Orbiter

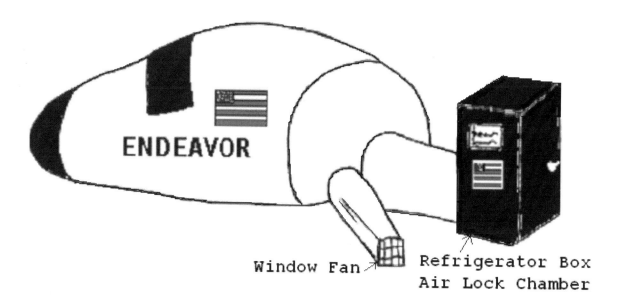

Window Fan   Refrigerator Box
Air Lock Chamber

Construction of a ½ Scale Model of the Shuttle Cabin

Materials:
1. 5 – 8 rolls of clear, plastic tape
2. White or clear plastic (available at a plant nursery)
3. Black plastic (available at hardware stores)
4. Scissors
5. String
6. Markers
7. Tape measure
8. Yardstick (or a very large straight edge)
9. Square window fan (works the best)
10. Refrigerator box (or any large box)
11. Exactor knife to cut refrigerator box (box cutter)
12. Extension cord for window fan
13. Chair or some device to keep the fan from falling over
14. Wire for air lock chamber door handle
15. Construction paper to make U.S. flag and door decorations
16. Glue stick for U.S. flag (if needed)
17. Large open area

Directions:
1. You will need a large area to build the orbiter. Assemble all the materials before you begin. Cut a piece of white plastic (polyethylene film) 23 ft. 11 in. x 10 ft. 9 in. Spread the plastic **Sheet (A)** flat on the floor. Cut an isosceles triangle template out of cardboard with a base of 12 in. and a height of 6 ft. 9 in. Use this template to outline 12 triangles on the length of the polyethylene film. Each triangle should be 13 in. apart. Using a black marker, measure and draw the triangles as indicated in **Diagram 25.** Cut out the twelve triangles and discard.

SHEET (A)

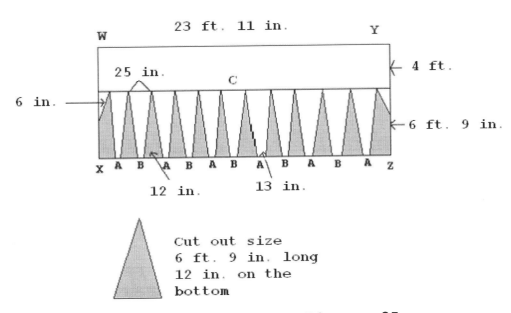

Diagram 25

2. Overlapping the edges slightly (½ in), tape AC to BC. Repeat until all twelve triangles have been connected.

*Note - Always tape the plastic on both sides (inside and outside for a stronger bond).

3. Tape WX to YZ. You should now have a cylinder with ends open. **See Diagram 26.**

Sheet (A)

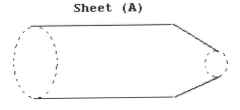

Diagram 26

89

*Note – For my space shuttle I used 24 ft. wide, white plastic donated from a plant nursery in North Carolina, Chappell Nursery. The plant nursery used the white plastic to cover plants during cold weather and frost. After talking to the owner of the store and telling him what I was going to do with the plastic for educational purposes, he donated all the plastic I needed for the shuttle. I offered to purchase the plastic from him, but he refused and as a result of his kindness, I named the first space shuttle cabin after his store…**USS Chappell.**

4. **Cutting the remaining sections of the shuttle:**
   - Cut a strip of white plastic into an 8 ft. x 4 ft. section labeled **Sheet (B) - Diagram 27** (fan tunnel).
   - Cut a 4 ft. x 4 ft. section of black plastic labeled **Sheet(C) – Diagram 28** (nose cone).
   - Cut a square of white plastic into an 8 ft. x 8 ft. section labeled **Sheet (D) - Diagram 29** (back of the shuttle orbiter).
   - Cut a strip of white plastic into an 8 ft. x 6 ft. section labeled **Sheet (E) - Diagram 30** (entry tunnel).

8 ft. x 4 ft.

Fan Tunnel

Sheet (B)

Diagram 27

4 ft. x 4 ft.

Nose Cone

Sheet (C)

Diagram 28

8 ft. x 8 ft.

Rear Circle

Sheet (D)

Diagram 29

8 ft. x 6 ft.

Entry Tunnel

Sheet (E)

Diagram 30

5. Make the nose cone from the 4 ft. x 4 ft. black square **Sheet (C)** - **Diagram 31.** Locate the center of the sheet by folding it into quarters. Tie a marker to a 2 ft. long string. Holding the other end of the string at the center, draw a circle having a radius of two feet. Cut out the circle.

(C)

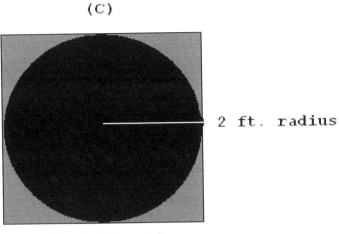

2 ft. radius

Black Plastic
Diagram 31

6. Cut out 10 triangles, 2 inches at the base of the circle and 12 in. long. Tape the triangle sides together as you did for the shuttle body - **Diagram 32.** Tape the nose cone to the small end of the shuttle body **(A).** ***Note** - This will not be neat…make it fit - **Diagram 33.** ***Note** - Remember to tape both sides of the plastic for a stronger bond.

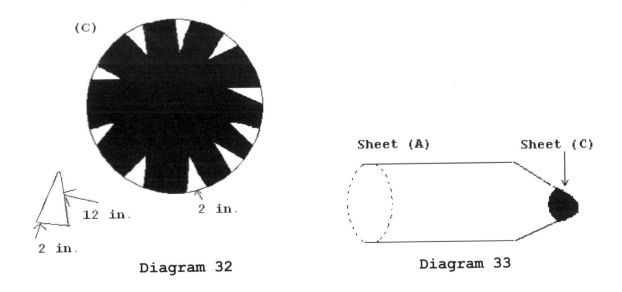

(C)

12 in.   2 in.

2 in.

Diagram 32

Sheet (A)   Sheet (C)

Diagram 33

7. Make the final cabin wall from the 8 ft. x 8 ft. white square **Sheet (D)**. Use a piece of string, 4 ft. long, and a marker to make a circle having a radius of 4 ft. (same method you used for making the nose cone circle). **See Diagram 34**. After cutting out the circle, tape it to the large open end of the shuttle. **See Diagram 35**.

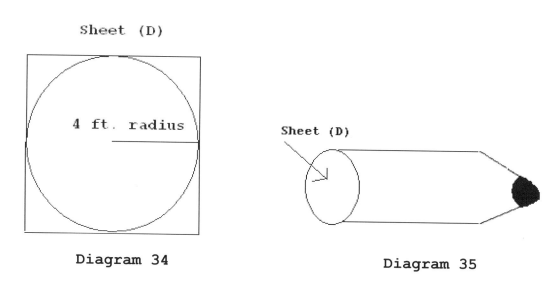

Diagram 34   Diagram 35

8. In the large circle, **Sheet (D)**, cut a "square" (the size of your window fan) just about 8 in. from the bottom on the left or right side of the circle, depending on which side you want to place your fan. **See Diagram 36**. Insert a sleeve in the hole made by taping the edges of **Sheet (B)** together. Tape side **AC** to side **BD** overlapping as needed to allow your fan to fit snugly in the outside end. **See Diagram 37**. Tape the plastic onto the window fan. Your set up should look something like **Diagram 38**.

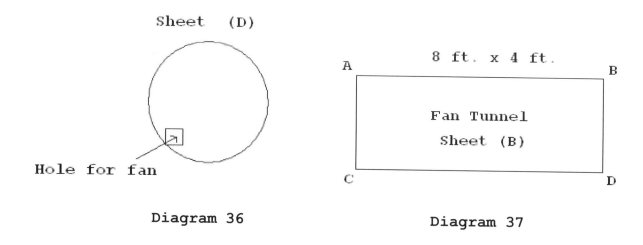

Diagram 36   Diagram 37

92

Sheet (D)

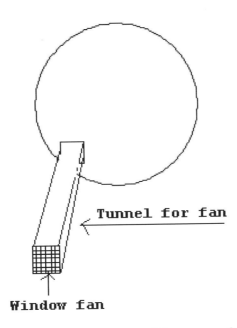

Diagram 38

*Note - You may now inflate the shuttle cabin and mark the position for the doorway.

9. Make the sleeve for the entry tunnel as you did for the fan using the 8 ft. x 6 ft. section labeled **Sheet (E)**. **See Diagram 39.** Install this sleeve in the back or side of the shuttle.

Sheet (D)

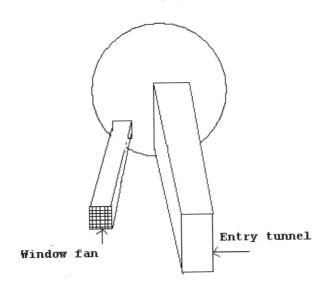

Diagram 39

10. You will need some way to stop the air from flowing out of the space shuttle. A refrigerator box (or any large box) makes a great airlock chamber. ***Note** – A card table may also be used. Put cardboard around the three front edges and tape the tunnel to the back of the table. Make a doorway in the front of the card table for entry. The students will have to crawl under the table into the tunnel.

11. Line the outside of the box in black plastic and decorate accordingly (e.g., Danger...airlock chamber). Make one side of the box a doorway to the outside and the opposite side the place where you will tape the entry tunnel. You will probably have to cut the refrigerator box halfway on the inside since the entry tunnel is not as tall as the box. Tape the white plastic to the inside of the box for the entry tunnel and then use wire to secure the outside door to keep it closed when the fan is in use. **See Diagram 40.**

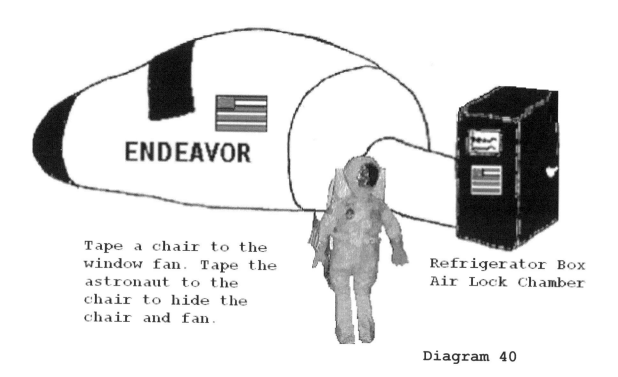

Tape a chair to the window fan. Tape the astronaut to the chair to hide the chair and fan.

Refrigerator Box Air Lock Chamber

Diagram 40

*Note – Once the students are inside the shuttle cabin their movement will cause pulling on the plastic and the fan might fall over and break. Always tape a chair to the outside of the fan for extra support so the fan won't fall over, hence the need for the standing stuffed-astronaut also tapped to the fan. The astronaut hides the fan and looks really cool. Always secure the fan to something that won't fall over. The orbiter deflates and rolls up for easy storage. Any tears the students make in the orbiter can easily be mended with clear tape. Never leave students unattended in the shuttle orbiter! ***Note** – The original directions for the larger shuttle given to me at a Science Teacher's Conference in North Carolina in 1996 were written by Renee Coward and Marianna Kesgen and adapted from Dr. Myra Halpin's book, <u>The Enterprise and Beyond</u>. The directions have been re-written and new graphs have been added for my classroom use. **For the extended directions for a full spacecraft (orbiter cabin, cargo bay, thrusters), see Appendix D, pages 226- 247. With permission from the Education Department of U.S. Space Camp, Huntsville, AL.**

Space Shuttle Activity Books from NASA

Download the following books from NASA using the provided web sites for activities and lessons to use along with your shuttle. Some of the manuals are over one hundred pages filled with all types of activities for students. For more information and help please contact:

Challenger Center for Space Science Education
1250 North Pitt Street
Alexandria, VA 22314
www.challenger.org
Phone: (703) 683-9740 - Fax: (703) 683-7546
© 2004 Challenger Center for Space Science Education

FREE DOWNLOADABLE   EDUCATIONAL RESOURCES!

- Comets
- Mars
- General Space
- International Space Station
- Shuttle
- Moon
- Solar System

"Challenger Center is committed to providing teachers with cutting-edge techniques to get students enthused about science and technology. We offer easily downloadable clipart and publications that can add visual excitement and hands-on activities to your lesson plan. When the subject is space, this is the place for news and resources to make every classroom minute count. Download all the resources you want from the subjects listed above!"

Space Shuttle Glider Kit - GRADES 5 - 12
The Space Shuttle Glider Kit was created by NASA.
http://www.challenger.org/tr/tr act set.htm

"This kit contains a model of the Space Shuttle glider at a 1:300 centimeters scale. Instructions for assembly and flying the model are included, as well as illustrations of the complete Shuttle Transportation System as it launches and lands. You will need the Adobe Acrobat reader view and print this document."

Microgravity Teacher's Guide - GRADES 5 – 12
Microgravity Teacher's Guide was created by NASA.
http://www.challenger.org/tr/tr act set.htm

"If you want to teach about principals of gravity and why it's useful to conduct laboratory experiments in an environment that minimizes the effects of gravity, you've come to the right place. This guide describes different ways to achieve microgravity, reasons why microgravity science is important, and includes activities on fluids, combustion, Materials: science, and biotechnology, all of which act differently when the effects of gravity are minimized. You will need the Adobe Acrobat reader view and print this document."

Suited For Spacewalking Teacher's Guide - GRADES 5 - 12
This publication was created by NASA
http://www.challenger.org/tr/tr act set.htm

"Your students all want to know how astronauts go to the bathroom in space. Don't you too? This teacher guide answers this and a lot of other questions about what it's like to live and work in space. In addition, the activities and demonstrations in this guide investigate the hostile environment of space and provides an overview of the evolution of spacesuit design and function. You will need the Adobe Acrobat reader view
and print this document."

Chapter 6

Endeavor Script

Because of time constraints of the space show, use only the last page of the script for the beginning act of the show.

Assign parts to:

1. **CAPCOM** (Mission Control Board on stage)
2. **Flight Director** (Mission Control Board on stage)
3. **Medical Officer**
4. **Weather Plane**
5. **Commander**
6. **Navigation**
7. **Lab #1**
8. **PAO #1**
9. **PAO #2**
10. **Pilot**
11. **Crew** - All other students sitting in the shuttle (Assign the last line of the play to all the rest of the students in the shuttle. They will yell the last line together.)

The show will open with all of the students in the space shuttle except for the two Mission Control Students – **CAPCOM and Flight Director** who will sit on stage at the Mission Control Board.

Two microphones will be needed. Place one microphone at the Mission Control Board and put one microphone inside the orbiter. The students in the orbiter will pass the microphone around to each student speaking his/her part. Have the students inside the orbiter sit in order of their speaking parts. Place the students who will yell the last line together so they can easily use the microphone. Select one student to hold the microphone for the "crew" as they yell into it.

Have a clue word from you to let the students know that it is time for the Medical Officer to start the reading of the play. I would always say, **"Look, the Endeavor is about to land. Let's listen. Take it away, Endeavor."** Point to the orbiter and walk to the side of stage, or something to that affect. You can use your own signal for the start of the play.

After the landing play the students will exit the orbiter one at a time. You will need to have a parent/teacher volunteer to open the air lock chamber of the shuttle, or you can go over and do it yourself. The Commander will exit first. Mission control will stand up as the students exit. The students will come out of the orbiter walk to the center of the stage, stop, and salute Mission Control. Mission Control will return the salute. Then the student will walk over to his/her pre-assigned chair on stage and stand "at ease" (military at ease formation-hands behind back) facing the space ship and with his/her back to the audience. The students will wait until the entire crew has exited the orbiter.

When all the students are standing at their chairs the Commander will yell, **"Attention!"** All the students will stand at attention – dropping their hands to their sides in a slapping motion. The Commander will yell, **"About face!"** All the students will turn to the right and stand facing the audience. The Commander will yell, **"At Ease!"** The students will return to the "at ease stance" – with hands behind their backs. The Commander will yell, **"You may be seated!"** All students take their seats. After the students are seated, start the show and the magic tricks.

*Note - I have done the landing script with first graders learning the entire script. Most of them memorized their lines, but I always made them use their own copy (with their names on it) for the actual show. They will practice really hard and will do a great job.

*Note – The landing script was given to me at a Science Teacher's Conference in North Carolina in 1996.

ENDEAVOR SCRIPT

PAO #1: This is the Public Affairs Officer at Ground Control. The final countdown for STS-79. The ground crew has begun filling the liquid-oxygen tank and the liquid-hydrogen tank in the external tank. The astronauts have entered the orbiter through the access hatch and are stowing their gear. We are now at T -1 hour, 50 minutes to liftoff.

LAUNCH CTRL: Endeavor, this is Launch Control. Radio check, over.

COMMANDER: Roger, out.

CAPCOM: Endeavor, this is Mission Control. Radio check, over.

COMMANDER: Roger, out.

LAUNCH CONTROL: Endeavor, this is Launch Control. Ready abort advisory check.

LAB #1: Roger, check is satisfactory, out.

CAPCOM: Endeavor, this is Control. Side hatch is secure.

LAB #2: Roger, we copy.

PAO #1: The ground crew has closed and secured the hatch.

MEDICAL #1: Control, this is Endeavor. We show normal cabin pressure, over.

CAPCOM: Roger, out.

PAO #2: Both cabin vent switches have been closed. We are now at T -1 hour, 5 minutes to liftoff.

PILOT: Control, this is Endeavor, Inertial measurement alignment complete. We show two-five degrees, fifty-four minutes, five seconds north, by 97 degrees, 29 minutes, 50 seconds west, over.

NAVIGATION: Roger, Endeavor. Out.

PAO #1: Latitude and longitude of launch pad 39-A has been confirmed.

LAB #2: Control, this is Endeavor. Boiler control switch ON. Nitrogen supply switch ON, over.

CAPCOM: Roger, out.

PILOT: Control, this is Endeavor. General-purpose computer, backup flight system complete.

CAPCOM: Roger, out.

PAO #2: The main flight software and its backup have been loaded at T -30 minutes to liftoff.

CAPCOM: Endeavor, this is Control. Ground Crew is secure, over.

COMMANDER: Roger, out.

LAB #1: Control, this is Endeavor. OMS pressure *ON* … Cabin vent complete, over.

CAPCOM: Roger, we see that, out.

COMMANDER: Control, this is Endeavor. Commander's voice check, over.

CAPCOM: Roger, out.

PILOT: Control, this is the pilot, voice check, over.

PAO #2: The commander and pilot have conducted voice checks with Mission Control Center. The vent valves have been closed. We are now at T -21 minutes to liftoff.

PILOT: Control, this is Endeavor. Flight plan is loaded into the computer, over.

CAPCOM: Roger, out.

PILOT: Control, I have entered SPEC99 and OPS101 into and the GPC, over.

CAPCOM: Roger, Endeavor. We confirm

LAUNCH CONTROL: Endeavor, this is Control. We will conduct the abort check, over

LAB #2: Roger. Looks good, out

MEDICAL #2: Control, what are the current weather conditions

METEOROLOGIST: M.E. 1, do you copy? What is your status

M.E. 1: We are orbiting Kennedy Space Center at 54,000 feet, over

COMMANDER: M.E. 1, this is Endeavor. What are the current weather conditions over KSC? Over

M.E. 1: Endeavor, this is M.E. 1. Temperature is at 60 degrees Fahrenheit. Humidity is at 65%. Winds are out of the SW at 5 mph, gusts to 10 mph., over

PILOT: M.E. 1, this is Endeavor. We copy, out

PAO #2: Weather conditions have been given at T -10 minutes to liftoff

MEDICAL #1: Control, this is Endeavor. Event timer started

CAPCOM: Roger, Endeavor. Out

PAO #1: The EVENT TIME indicator has started and is now counting down. The automatic ground launch sequencer has started. The crew access arm has retracted at T -7 minutes to liftoff.

LAUNCH CTRL: Endeavor, this is Control. Begin APU prestart procedure, over

LAB #2: Roger, out

PAO #2: The auxiliary power unit controller power switches are all ON at T -6 minutes to liftoff

PILOT: Control, this is Endeavor. Prestart complete. Powering up APU'S, over

CAPCOM: APU's look good, out

LAUNCH CTRL: Endeavor, this is Control. You are on internal power, over

COMMANDER: Roger, out

PAO #2: The Orbiter has switched to internal power at T − 4 minutes. 30 seconds to liftoff

CAPCOM: Endeavor, this is Control. Hydraulic check complete, over

LAB #1: Roger, out

CAPCOM: Endeavor, this is Control. Main engine gimbal complete, over

LAB #2: Roger, out

PAO #1: The Orbiter main engines have swiveled to their launch positions at T −2 minutes, 55 seconds to liftoff.

CAPCOM: Endeavor, this is Control. O-two vents closed. Looks good, out

MEDICAL #1: Roger, out

PAO #2: The external tank oxygen vents have been closed; the liquid-oxygen tank has begun pressurizing at T −2 minutes to liftoff

COMMANDER: Control, this is Endeavor. APU to inhibit, over

CAPCOM: Roger, we copy Endeavor. Out

PAO #2: The audio volume control has been adjusted. The auxiliary power units have been set to INHIBIT.

LAUNCH CTRL: Medical Specialist, report on the condition of the crew, over

MEDICAL #2: Control, this is Endeavor. The crew is in excellent condition

CAPCOM: Roger, Endeavor. Out

LAUNCH CTRL: Endeavor, this is Control. H-two tank pressurization OK. You are go for launch, over

LAB #1: Roger, go for launch, over

CAPCOM: Endeavor, this is Control. APU start is go. You are on your on-board computer, over.

LAB #1: Roger, out.

LAUNCH CTRL: 15, 14, 13, 12, 11, 10, 9, 8, 7, 6, 5, 4...

PAO #1: LIFT OFF!! The Endeavor has cleared the tower. Lift-off.

CAPCOM: The tower has been cleared. All engines look good. Beginning roll maneuver. Roll maneuver complete. Endeavor, you're looking good. We are now switching control from Kennedy to Houston.

PILOT: Control, this is Endeavor. Main engines at 65%. Over.

CAPCOM: Roger, out.

COMMANDER: Control, this is Endeavor. Max Q, over.

CAPCOM: Roger. Endeavor. Out.

PILOT: Control, this is Endeavor. We have SRB burnout; ready for SRB sep, over.

CAPCOM: Roger, out.

COMMANDER: Control, this is Endeavor. We have SRB sep, over.

CAPCOM: Roger, we can see that, Endeavor. Out.

PAO #1: The solid rocket boosters have separated from the Orbiter at T + 2 minutes, 7 seconds.

FLIGHT DIRECTOR: Endeavor, you are negative return. Do you copy?

LAB #2: Roger, Mission Control. Negative return, out.

LAB #1: Control, this is Endeavor. We are single engine press to MECO, over.

CAPCOM: Roger, Endeavor, out.

FLIGHT DIRECTOR: Endeavor, this is Control. Main engine throttle down, over

PILOT: Roger, out

FLIGHT DIRECTOR: Endeavor, this is Control. Go for main engine cut-off, over.

COMMANDER: Roger Main engine cut-off on schedule, out.

PAO #2: The three main engines have shut down.

FLIGHT DIRECTOR: Endeavor, this is Control. Go for ET separation.

LAB #1: Roger, we have external tank sep, over.

PAO #1: The external tank has separated from the Orbiter.

PILOT: Beginning minus Z translation, out.

PAO #1: The crew are preparing for orbital maneuvering system burn number one.

CAPCOM: Endeavor, this is Control. You are go for OMS -1 burn, over.

LAB #2: Roger, OMS-1, out.

PILOT: Control, this is Endeavor. We have OMS cut-off, over.

CAPCOM: Roger, we copy.

COMMANDER: Umbilical doors closed, over.

CAPCOM: Roger, out.

FLIGHT DIRECTOR: Endeavor, this is Control. Coming up on OMS-2, over.

LAB #1: Roger, OMS-2.

PILOT: OMS-2 cut-off. We have achieved orbit, over.

CAPCOM: Roger, Endeavor, out. Congratulations! You're really looking good out there.

FLIGHT DIRECTOR: Endeavor, begin on-orbit operations.

COMMANDER: Roger, Control. Out.

**********BEGIN MISSIONS EXPERIMENTS HERE****************

FLIGHT DIRECTOR: Endeavor, prepare to close cargo bay doors, over.

LAB #1: Roger, Control. Ready to close PBD'S, over.

CAPCOM: Closing PBD's...PBD's closed and locked.

COMMANDER: Roger, Control.

PAO #1: The astronauts have closed the payload bay doors.

COMMANDER: Mission Control, this is Endeavor. APU prestart complete, over.

PAO #2: The astronauts have finished powering up auxiliary power units.

FLIGHT DIRECTOR: Roger out. M.E. 1 this is Mission Control. What is your position?

WEATHER PLANE: We are orbiting KSC at 54,000 feet and are ready to trail Endeavor in, over.

FLIGHT DIRECTOR: Roger. M.E. 1.

PAO #1: The Fight Director has contacted the NASA weather plane, M.E. I, to verify its position and status.

FLIGHT DIRECTOR: Endeavor, you are go for de-orbit burn, over.

COMMANDER: Roger, go for de-orbit burn, out.

PILOT: Beginning altitude adjustment. Maneuver to burn altitude complete. Descending into the upper atmosphere, over.

MEDICAL OFFICER: ME. 1, this is Endeavor. What are the current weather conditions over KSC? Over.

WEATHER PLANE: Endeavor, this is M.E. I. Current weather conditions are winds out of the north/northwest at 15 knots with gusts to 25 knots; partly cloudy from 10,000 feet to 25,000 feet with unlimited visibility above 25,000 feet. Barometric pressure at 38.6 and rising. Chance for rain at 20 percent.

PAO #2: The NASA weather plane, ME. 1, has reported the current weather conditions. Conditions for landing are nominal.

LAB #2: M.E. I, this is Endeavor. We copy, over.

FLIGHT DIRECTOR: Commander, you will enter communications blackout in 20 seconds, over.

COMMANDER: Roger, Control. Communications blackout confirmed, over. *(To shuttle crew)* Entering Blackout.

PAO #1: The shuttle has entered a region of intense ionization that prohibits radio communications.

MISSION CONTROL WILL NOW TURN OFF RADIOS. COMMUNICATION BLACKOUT IN EFFECT. COMMUNICATION IN ORBITER ONLY

PILOT: Activating RCS roll thrusters. Adjusting altitude for re-entry.

LAB #2: External heating 600 degrees.

PILOT: RCS thrusters deactivating.

LAB # 1: External heating 900 degrees.

COMMANDER: Extend elevators. Conduct first roll reversal.

*SHUTTLE CREW You have now left the region of high ionization and may resume communication with Mission

Control. GROUND CONTROL WILL NOW RECEIVE SIGNAL TO TURN RADIOS BACK ON*

MEDICAL OFFICER: Leaving Communications blackout, Control, do you read? Over.

FLIGHT DIRECTOR: We read you, Endeavor. We also have visual contact. You are looking good, over.

PAO #2: The shuttle has left the region of high ionization and has resumed communications with Mission Control.

PILOT: Control, this is Endeavor. We are ready to assume manual control, over.

FLIGHT DIRECTOR: Roger, Endeavor. Deactivating computer guidance systems. Happy landings, over.

PAO #1: The pilot will now take control of the flight controls and land the shuttle manually.

PILOT: Roger, Control. First roll reversal complete.

LAB #2: Temperature 1300 degrees and climbing.

CAPCOM: M.E. 1, this is Mission Control. Do you have the Endeavor in sight? Over.

WEATHER PLANE: Control, this is M.E. 1. We have the Endeavor in sight, approximately 3 miles downrange. We are closing distance, over.

LAB #1: Temperature 1500 degrees and falling.

NAVIGATION: Endeavor, this is Control. Set speed brakes to 100%, over.

COMMANDER: Roger, Control. Speed brakes to 100%, over.

PAO #2: The shuttle's speed brakes have been set to maximum to slow the shuttle's rate of descent.

PILOT: Conducting second roll reversal.

***Use these last pages for the Landing Play**

NAME _____

MEDICAL OFFICER: Temperature nominal. Deploying air data probes.

WEATHER PLANE: Endeavor, your Current ground air speed is Mach 3.3, over.

COMMANDER: Roger. Mach 3.3. Out.

NAVIGATION: Endeavor, landing gear, over.

LAB #1: Roger, Control, this is Control. Deploy Landing gear deployed, over.

PAO #1: The landing gear of the shuttle has been lowered.

NAVIGATION: M.E. 1, this is Control. Confirm deployed and locked gear, over.

WEATHER PLANE: Control, this is M.E. 1. Gear down and locked. Out.

PAO #2: M.E. 1 the NASA weather plane, confirms that the shuttle's landing gear are down and locked.

COMMANDER: Control, confirm flight auto-land guidance systems active, over.

CAPCOM: Endeavor, this is Control. Auto-land system active.

PILOT: Roger, Control. Out.

NAVIGATION: Endeavor touchdown. Repeat, you have rear wheel touchdown. Nose wheel touchdown...Repeat, you have nose wheel touchdown.

PILOT: Braking procedure active.

COMMANDER: Full stop...We have full stop.

NAVIGATION: M.E. 1, this is Control. Confirm full stop of Endeavor. Over.

WEATHER PLANE: Control, this is M.E. 1. Endeavor is at full stop.

NAVIGATION: M.E. 1, this is Control. Thank you, and you are cleared on corridor 3 heading 285. You are cleared to 40.000 feet, over.

WEATHER PLANE: Roger, Control. Leaving area on corridor 3, clear to 40.000 feet. Over.

FLIGHT DIRECTOR: Endeavor, you are cleared to release safety harness, over.

COMMANDER: Roger, Control. Releasing safety harness.

FLIGHT DIRECTOR: You are cleared to egress the shuttle. Welcome home, Endeavor.

COMMANDER: Roger, Control. We are egressing shuttle. Endeavor Out.

CREW: Houston, We're home!

Chapter 7

Space Camp T-Shirts

U.S. Space Camp in Huntsville, Alabama let all of the International Teachers of the Year, attending the ten-day camp, keep their blue flight suits. Wearing a flight suit as the presenter of the show makes the production more aesthetically pleasing to the students. Flight suits can be purchased from the Space Camp web site at **www.spacecamp.com**.

Adult Flight Suit   **Price: $75.00**

* Web site description – "Wear a suit like the astronauts wear! The blue suit comes with 5 patches: U.S. Space Camp, NASA Visitors Center, U.S. Flag, NASA Vector, and Shuttle Program. The green suit comes with 2 patches: Aviation Challenge and U.S. Flag. Each suit also has a velcro patch for a leather name badge. Available in S, M, L, XL, XXL, XXXL. NAME BADGE OPTIONAL"

Space Camp has given their permission for you to make T-Shirts for your students using the Space Camp patches on the above flight suit. The enclosed patches can be copied or colored with permanent markers and taped onto a T-Shirt.

There are two sets of patches on the following pages. One set is used as the model for coloring the patches since this is a black-and-white book. You can use these patches if you go over them with a permanent magic marker to add some color, which is what I used for my shows. Copy them, color over them, cut them out and tape them onto a T-Shirt. The other set of patches can be colored by your students using permanent markers, cut out and taped onto a T-Shirt.

Choose the set of patches you would like to use, cut them out and tape them on a white or blue T-Shirt using two-inch clear tape. See the large diagram on the next page for placement of patches on T-Shirt.

Each student is assigned a role in the show according to the script for the *Endeavor Landing Play*. Put the student's role in the show or "title" in the play, on the back of the shirt to make the T-Shirt look more official and for them to be able to identify their shirt easily (e.g., CAPCOM, PAO #1). ***Note** – Keep the T-Shirts until time for the show to make sure they are nice and clean. The students love to wear them and if you don't keep them before the show, the shirts will get soiled.

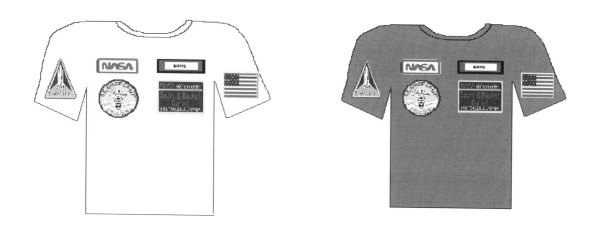

Where to put patches

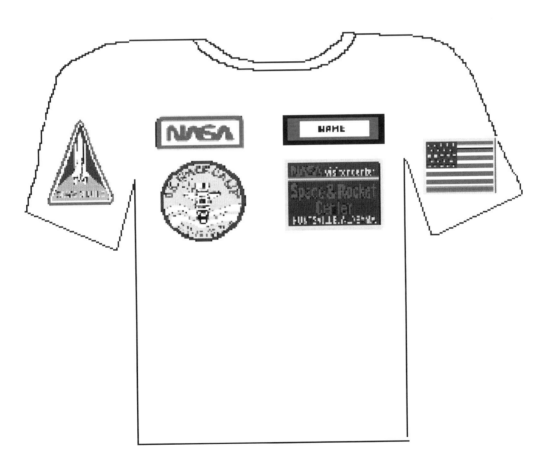

Front of T-Shirt

Back of T-Shirt (Roles in the production)

Patches to Color with Permanent Marker

Place on right front of T-Shirt

Name Tag – Write in name and place on left front of T-Shirt

Place on left arm of T-Shirt

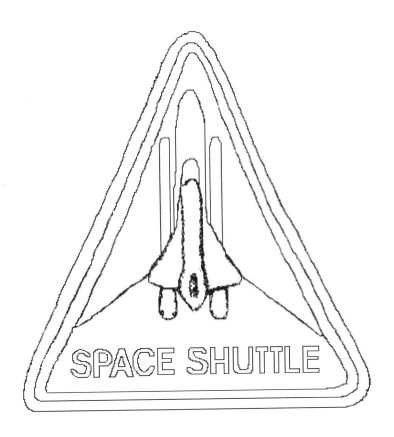

Place on right arm of T-Shirt

Place on left side of T-Shirt

Place on right front of T-Shirt

Colored Patches

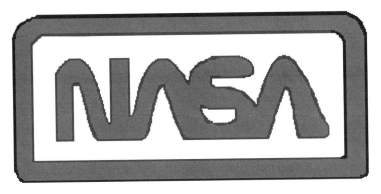

Place on right front of T-Shirt

Red   Red

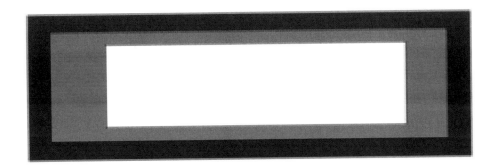

Write in name and place on left side of T-Shirt

Red

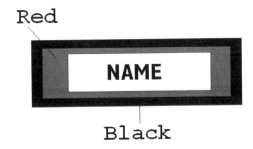

Black

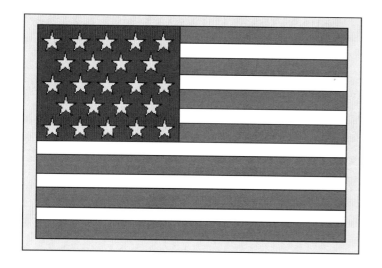

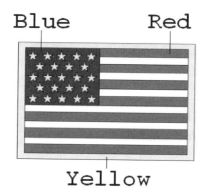

Blue   Red

Yellow

Place on left arm of T-Shirt

Dk.
Blue

Red

Lt.
Blue

Yellow

Place on right arm of T-Shirt

118

Red   Blue

Yellow

Place on left side of T-Shirt

Red   Dk. Blue

Lt. Blue   Yellow

Place on right front of T-Shirt

T-SHIRT
Back of Shirt Titles

See Appendix B - Copy, cut and tape the titles onto back of T-Shirts (pages 206 - 217)

ALIEN #1

ME TOO - ALIEN #2

CAPCOM

Flight Director

Medical Officer

Weather Plane

Commander

Navigation

Lab #1

PAO #1

PAO #2

Pilot

Mission Control - Assign this part to any volunteer or parent helper you might have in the show.

Crew - Assign this part to all other students in the class and number consecutively (e.g., Crew #1, Crew # 2, Crew # 3, Crew #4).

Example of students in Space Camp T-Shirt Uniforms

Materials:
1. White or blue T-Shirts
2. Copies of Space Camp Patches
3. Clear, white tape
4. Scissors
5. Permanent markers if needed

Where is Goo Goo?

Chapter 8

Student Scientific Quotes

The presentation is an interactive show in which the children, teachers and parents in the audience come up on stage and participate in the experiments. Having your students on stage either reading or memorizing a scientific fact in front of the audience is a way for your students to star in the show and it also gives them a chance to practice public speaking skills at an early age.

Practice the experiments before hand in your classroom with your students so they will be familiar with the experiments and will know what will happen during the show. Practicing with your students will let you work out any kinks in the procedures that you might have trouble with on stage.

Since your students will have already seen and done the experiments in the classroom that will be used in the presentation, use your students as facilitators for the show. During various parts of the show direct the students to go out into the audience and choose volunteers to participate in the experiments.

At the needed times during the show, call on certain students and tell them specifically how many students to bring from the audience at a specific time **(e.g., "Wesley, please choose three students from the audience. Courtney, please choose five students.")**. You can easily control your students by putting the student names on the show manifest. That will tell you exactly whom to call and how many participants they need to pick. ***Note –** See the **"Show Manifest"** for the exact example (page 1).

After the *Endeavor Landing Play* the students should sit on the stage in assigned seating. They should wait until you call them by name to go out into the audience. After picking the selected number of students, parents or teachers you request of them, they should return to their seats and wait for you to call them again to introduce themselves and read their scientific quote.

Depending on the age of the students in the production, the student quotes can be as easy or advanced as you want. At certain times during the show, call three students to come up to the center of the stage (a microphone will be needed – use the microphone from the Mission Control Board) and introduce themselves and read a scientific quote to the audience one at a time. This way your students will have the chance to speak in public and be the star of the show for a few moments **(e.g., "Hello, my name is Wesley. Did you know that a moon is a solid**

body that orbits a planet? Moons are also called satellites."). As the student leaves the microphone, he/she should give you back their quote card.

Put the quotes on a piece of 9 in. x 6 in. construction paper. Below are examples of my second grade – Student Quotes.

Wesley	A-1

Did you know that a moon is a solid body that orbits a planet? Moons are also called satellites.

Taylor	A-2

Venus has the longest "day" of any of our planets. Venus' day lasts 243 days, which is 18 days longer than its year.

Joseph	A-3

The Great Red Spot on Jupiter is a tremendous never-ending storm, similar to a hurricane on Earth.

Ryan	B-1

When the space shuttle Challenger took off in 1983, Sally Ride was on board. She was the first American woman in space.

The first group of three students you will call onstage should have the sequencing numbers of A-1, A-2, and A-3. The second group of students should have the numbers of B-1, B-2 and B-3 and so forth. Sequencing the students in this order will make practicing easier in the classroom. Keep the student cards on the stage table in alphabetical order (so the students won't lose them). It will be very easy for you to hand them to the students as they step up to the microphone.

After practicing for the show, the cards will always be mixed up. Give one of your students the job of putting the cards back into the correct order, another way for them to practice sequencing.

Materials:
1. Colored, construction paper
2. White, paper for quotes
3. Scissors
4. Glue stick

Here are some student quotes for a second grade class; however the possibilities are endless. Try to put some comedy into the quotes to make the audience laugh.

- Jupiter's moon, Ganymede, is the largest moon in the solar system. It is almost as large as the planet, Pluto.

- Many of the moon's craters were caused by giant asteroids, the size of Rhode Island and Delaware, which fell on the moon millions of years ago.

- Why is a rocket like a jellyfish? Both are jet propelled. Each moves forward as a jet shoots out in the opposite direction. In a jellyfish, the jet is a stream of water. In a rocket, it is a stream of gas that comes from exploding fuel.

- Our moon's temperature changes drastically. When the sun is overhead, the moon's temperature is 243 degrees F (117 degrees C). By nightfall, the temperature drops to -261 degrees F (-163 degrees C).

- There are nine planets in our solar system. The closest planet to the sun is called Mercury and the farthest from the sun is called Pluto.

- What is full of holes yet doesn't leak? A wet handkerchief. It doesn't leak because the water forms a film between the threads of the cloth. This film is strong enough to hold the water in.

- What heavenly body has a head and a tail? A comet. The head, the main part, is probably made of frozen water and ammonia, dry ice, pieces of stone and metal and dust. It is sometimes like a big, dirty snowball that shines because it reflects sunlight. As it comes near the sun, the ice turns to vapor, forming a tail of gases.

- Sunlight on Uranus is 400 times weaker than sunlight on Earth.

- Over two million pounds of meteors shower down onto Earth everyday. Most of them burn up in Earth's atmosphere before they reach us.

- When is a meteor not a meteor? When it has landed on Earth. Then it is called a meteorite.

- Saturn is encircled by thousands of thin rings that change everyday. These rings are made of particles ranging in size from dust to giant boulders.

- Jupiter is our sun's largest satellite. It is larger that all the planets and their moons combined.

- Where in the world is there no down, only up? At the center of the Earth. From that point, there is no direction to go but up.

- Saturn's winds blow 1,100 miles per hour. Saturn's winds are up to 15 times more powerful than a hurricane and up to 30 times more powerful than a tornado.

- A lady was served a glassful of water, but she couldn't drink it. Why not? The glass was full of ice. The water was frozen.

- What is the easiest way to make a fire with two sticks? Make sure one of them is a match.

- When is half a moon not a half a moon? When it's a full moon. What we call the full moon is the side that we see, fully lighted. Actually, it is a half of the moon. The other side of the moon is the half we never see.

- When do you see sunshine at night? When you see moonlight. The moon has no light of its own. It shines because it reflects the sunlight that hits its surface.

- The most distant stars in our galaxy are estimated to be 63,000 light-years away. This distance equals 16 billion trips around Earth.

- Though Halley's Comet is made mostly of ice, the comet's temperature was 85 degrees F (30 degrees C) when it whizzed past Earth in 1986.

Chapter 9

Mission Control Board

To give the show an authentic look, along with the orbiter, I created a mock Mission Control Board using cardboard, construction paper, space pictures, tape and Christmas lights. I purchased some cordless walkie-talkies from Walmart and had the two students from the *Endeavor Landing Play* sit on stage at the control panel while they read their parts for the play.

Materials:
 1. 2 - 3 rolls of clear, plastic tape
 2. Scissors
 3. Exactor knife to cut cardboard
 4. Markers and a pencil
 5. Colored, construction paper
 6. Red, Christmas lights
 7. White, Christmas lights
 8. Space pictures
 9. Extension cord
10. Roll of black paper
11. Colored copies of the U.S. Space Camp, T-Shirt patches

My first attempt at making a control board was very simple and was limited by the size of the boxes I could find. You can make the board as large or as small as you like.

Using the board in the show, you will need an extension cord, an electrical outlet and a microphone for the students.

One of my students brought in an old keyboard and we attached the cord to the control board and he typed on the keyboard like he was sending messages to the shuttle. See picture above.

Instructions:

1. Cover the front side of a large cardboard box with black construction paper (5 ft. x 3 ft x 6 in.). The box can be cut down so the width of the board is about one-half foot.
2. Using clear tape, attach any space pictures you have on hand.
3. With a pencil or sharp object, poke holes in the cardboard around the pictures for the Christmas lights to go through.
4. From the back of the box, push the small lights through to the front side of the box. Tape the lights in place; otherwise they will fall out when you move the control board.
5. Use your imagination or have your students draw gauges and dials and attach to the board. Enclosed are samples of some gauges and dials you might use.
6. Upon completion, tape the back of the box shut and cover the back in black paper.
7. To make the board sturdy, attach two triangle shaped pieces of cardboard to the back of the box to help the control board stand up by itself.

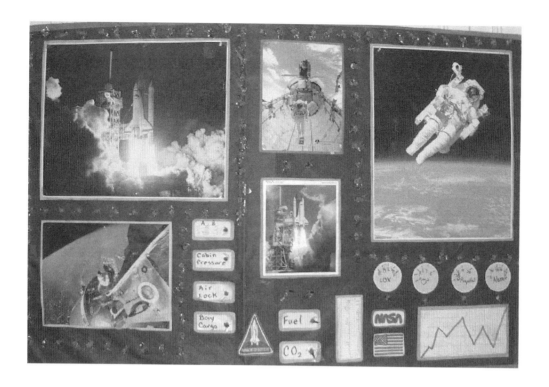

    Above is an example of my last control board. The board can also be made out of pegboard using real dials, gauges and switches. The above picture should give you a good example of what to do. Let your students be creative and come up with some good ideas.

Example of stage set up and Mission Control Board.

DIALS & GAUGES
The circle marks the place for the red light.

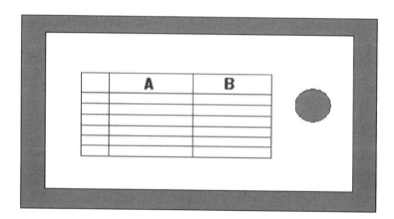

Fill in some numbers or use part of a spreadsheet in this box.

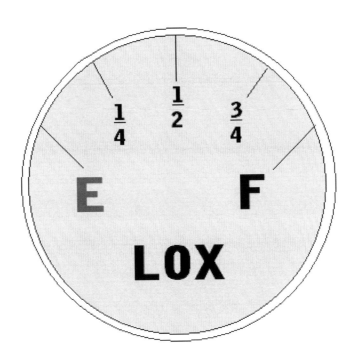

Liquid Oxygen Level

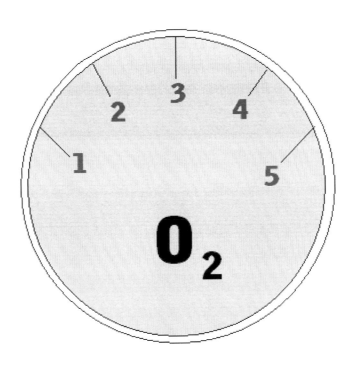

Oxygen Level

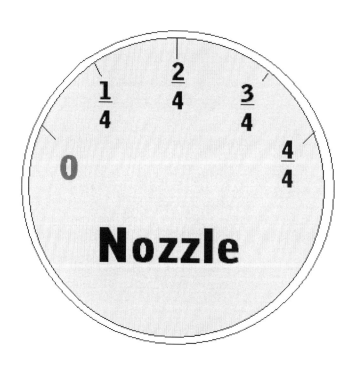

Turn graph sideways

Chapter 10

Aliens

Since one of my hobbies is doing stand-up comedy in nightclubs, I wanted to put some comedy into the show and one of my second graders suggested having an alien run around the space ship. For my very first show using second grade students, I made an alien mask out of cardboard and green/yellow construction paper. Using one of my husband's disposable white coveralls, I made an alien costume and the students made alien patches for the suit. The extra material had to be cut off of the arms and legs of the coveralls since my student was much smaller then the adult coverall. I used yellow, kitchen gloves for the hands. It was a bit difficult for the student to see out of the mask, and he complained that it was very hot inside of it. Air holes were needed to make it better for the student to breathe.

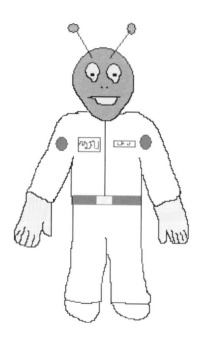

Materials:
1. Disposable coveralls
2. Yellow, kitchen gloves
3. Alien Patches
4. Pipe cleaners for the antennae
5. Construction paper - green, blue and yellow
6. Scissors
7. Clear tape
8. Red marker

The hardest decision for me was choosing one of the students to be the alien since all of them wanted the part. I had one girl who was dying to be the alien, but her behavior was not conducive to my classroom rules. When I chose another student to play the part of the alien, this little girl was very disappointed. I called her aside and had the "teacher-student" talk about improving her behavior and following the classroom rules. Well, needless to say, she was the model student for weeks and I wrote a part for another alien into the show and made another alien costume.

During the first part of the show, the aliens should be hidden from the audience. If you don't have a stage for the presentation or a place for the aliens to hide, then make two folding screens out of large cardboard boxes. Cover the screens with construction paper and have your students decorate the outside of them with space decorations. It's very important for the aliens to be hidden from the audience as not to spoil the element of surprise. It's also hard for the students dressed as aliens not to peek out at the audience since they love playing the part and want to scare the audience. Below is a picture of one of the simple screens I made in order to hide the aliens from the audience. Place the screens on either side of the stage so the aliens can run from one to the other.

It's a good idea to have two parent helpers' stay with the aliens and cue them on when to run out around the orbiter. Give each parent/teacher helper a copy of the show manifest so they will be able to watch for the times that the aliens are needed on stage. I also had "key words" for the aliens to listen for and know when to come out such as, **"My mission here today is to tell you that knowledge is power."** I would **yell** the word, **mission**, really loud and when the aliens heard me say the word, **mission, in a yelling voice** that would be the cue for them to run out. The word, **mission**, was the major cue word.

When I had chosen my two aliens, I did an impromptu in class and asked the taller alien, **"What's your name?"** He said, **"Goo Goo."** My students roared with laughter and I loved it. I turned to my students and said, **"Goo Goo?"** and made a face. They laughed again. I asked him, **"Where are you from, Goo Goo?"** He said, **"Goo Gone."** My students laughed some more. I knew it was going to work and a star was born. I wanted the smaller, girl alien, to just say, **Me Too**, to everything I asked her. I asked her, **"What's your name?"** She replied, **"Me Too!"** in a high squeaky voice. I asked, **"And are you from Goo Gone?"** She replied, **"Me Too!"** I then asked, **"So why are you here?"** Goo Goo replied, **"I want the Power!"** and Me Too replied, **"Me Too!"** Then I started the "I've Got the Power" music cassette and the two aliens started dancing around the class. My students were laughing so hard I knew it would work on stage.

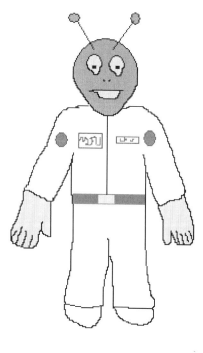

Goo Goo

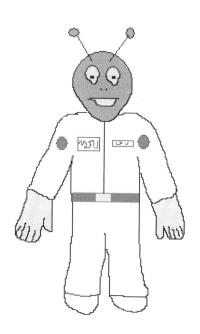

Me Too

To build the excitement of the aliens' presence, I had them come on stage three times during the presentation. Follow the show manifest to note the exact times and places that the aliens are needed. The aliens carried signs as they came across the stage and waved to the audience. The signs were numbered on the back, so it made it easier for the aliens to remember the correct sign to carry at the correct time.

When the cue was given for the aliens to come out, the alien, Goo Goo, walked out first carrying sign #1. He walked behind me so I wouldn't see him. The audience was surprised and yelled at me to look at the alien. After I waited until I was sure he was gone, I turned around and looked and said to the audience, "There is no such thing as aliens. I don't see any aliens." That was the cue for the alien, Me Too, to come out carrying her sign, which said, "Me Too." The audience yelled at me again and screamed about the alien. I waited, turned, looked and told the audience that I didn't see any aliens and continued with the next experiment.

After about four more experiments, I gave the cue again for the aliens to come out by yelling, "My **mission** here today is to tell you that **knowledge is power.**" The alien, Goo Goo, came out again carrying sign #2. I followed the same procedure of telling the audience that I didn't see any aliens and that there was no such thing as aliens. Then the alien, Me Too, came out carrying her sign. The second time the aliens appeared the roar of the crowd was much higher and they were screaming and yelling at me to look. It was awesome fun. I just acted like I didn't care and continued with the next experiment.

The third and last time the aliens came out was tremendous. The alien, Goo Goo, came out first with sign #3, and again I followed the same procedure. After Me Too came out with her sign and went around the orbiter, the aliens dropped their signs and crept out with their hands up in the air and stalked over to me.

The audience stood up and came out of their seats yelling at me to look at the aliens. The aliens each tapped me on my shoulders and I turned, looked, and screamed as if surprised. By now there was a great roar of laughter in the room.

Then I used a microphone and asked them who they were and where they were from. **See alien script (page 140).**

When the aliens said they wanted the power, I walked over and turned on the music and the aliens started dancing around. You may also have a volunteer turn on the music. I let them dance for a minute while the audience laughed, and then I said, "Shoo! Get off my stage and quit bothering us. You can't have our power. Shoo." I proceeded to shoo them off the stage while they danced off. It was then time for the next experiment.

At this time the aliens changed out of their costumes and joined the other students on stage.

The second time I did the presentation, I purchased two alien costumes from a costume shop in Las Vegas, so I didn't have to take the time to make the cardboard masks and coverall costumes. The purchased costumes were more realistic. I have had adult helpers play the role of the aliens, but the small costume didn't fit them, so we used black graduation robes as alien costumes and it worked just fine. The adults were able to wear the masks and the robes to make striking aliens.

At one of my presentations a smaller child was very afraid of the large aliens, then all of a sudden, he shouted, "Look at their shoes." The adults had on tennis shoes and his mother was able to convince him that it was only a costume, and then he smiled and loved it. That was one of the highlights of the show.

`Web sites for purchasing Alien costumes:`

`http://www.halloweenstreet.com/prod details/id-1703-action-detail`

$14.99

`http://www.kidders.com/alien-costume.htm`

$22.99

$5.79

Alien Script:

Teacher to Goo Goo: "Who are you?"

Goo Goo: "Goo Goo."

Teacher to audience: "Goo Goo?"

Teacher to Goo Goo: "Where are you from, Goo Goo?"

Goo Goo: "Goo Gone."

Teacher to audience: "Goo Gone?"

Teacher to Me Too: "What's your name?"

Me Too: "Me Too."

Teacher to audience: "Me Too."

Teacher to Me Too: "And are you from Goo Gone?"

Me Too: "Me Too."

Teacher to aliens: "What do you want? Why are you here?"

Goo Goo: "I want the power!"

Me Too: "Me Too."

(After the aliens dance around for a minute the teacher says:)

Teacher to the aliens: "Get out of here. You can't have our power. Shoo! Get off my stage and quit bothering us. Shoo, Get!"

Alien signs:

Me
Alien

Sign # 1 - Goo Goo

ALIENS
RULE

Sign # 2 - Goo Goo

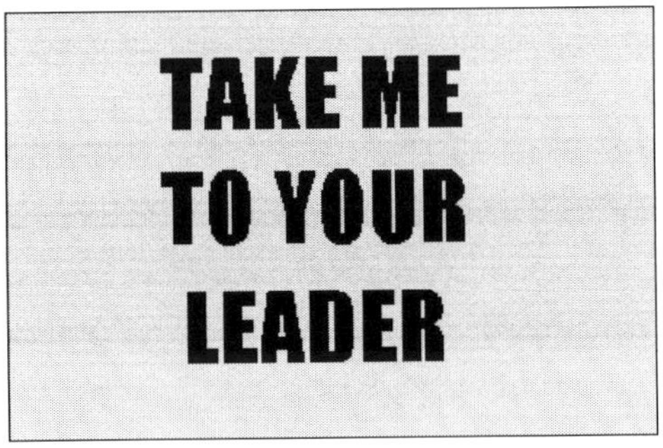

**TAKE ME
TO YOUR
LEADER**

Sign # 3 - Goo Goo

Me
Too

Me Too's only sign

Chapter 11

Astronaut Display

When I built the orbiter, I put the fan vent, the name of the shuttle and the American flag on the left side of the orbiter, which faced the audience (not realizing I did this). I didn't want the students to see the fan and the chair taped to the fan that was used for support, so I make a huge cardboard drawing of an astronaut. The drawing was taped to the front of the chair and the drawing actually accentuated the stage. For decoration, I taped an American Flag in the astronaut's hand. The students added some color to the astronaut, a cut out of the orbiter and a tin foil star on the cardboard.

Materials:
1. Piece of cardboard (box - 5 ft. x 2 ½ or 3 ft.)
2. Roll of black paper
3. Overhead projector
4. Colored markers
5. Scissors
6. Glue
7. Small, American flag
8. Clear tape
9. Tin foil
10. Space pictures

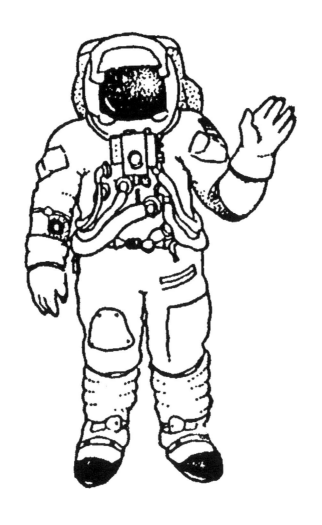

Make a copy of the above (clip art) astronaut on transparency film and use an overhead projector to enlarge it to the size you need for your standing, cardboard astronaut.

Another use for the astronaut would be to use him on a bulletin board. Take pictures of your students and enlarge their faces to fit behind the astronaut's mask. Make a student-size astronaut and cut out the mask part of the drawing. Tape a picture of a student's face behind the mask. Cover the face with plastic wrap if you like or leave the face uncovered. The students will love having a life-size copy of themselves as astronauts. You can also make smaller sized astronauts with the students' faces and put them on a bulletin board display. Decorate the outside wall of your classroom with the drawings.

Stuffed Astronaut:

The more times I performed the show the more I thought of ways to improve it. I ordered some disposable coveralls for my husband to use when he worked on the car from **American Scientific Surplus Catalog**. Seeing the white coveralls gave me the idea of an astronaut's suit for a stuffed figure.

http://www.sciplus.com/

Instructions:

1. To create the astronaut, take one of the cheap coveralls and stuff it with crumpled newspaper and old paper from the classroom to form the body.
2. Inflate a large balloon and cover it with white paper to make the head.
3. Add a facemask to the head by gluing tin foil on the front of the balloon.
4. Tape the head and body together using two-inch clear tape.
5. Buy a pair of gray, workman's gloves, stuff them with paper and tape them to the arms of the stuffed astronaut.
6. Make a set of the T-Shirt Space Camp patches, and tape them to the suit. **See Chapter 7 Space Camp T-Shirts, page 111.**
7. Make a cardboard oxygen tank, and tape it to the back of the astronaut. (Square box with fake tubing)
8. Use two cardboard boxes to shape into boots for the astronaut.
9. Tape a small American flag to one of the astronaut's hands.
10. Stand the astronaut up, and tape it to a small dolly so you can move the astronaut easily.
11. Place the astronaut on the dolly in front of the fan, and tape the fan to the dolly for support, so the students won't knock the fan over. ***Note** - After my third broken fan, I needed a way to make the fan more secure while the students were in the orbiter.
12. Drape a gold/silver solar blanket behind the astronaut to hide the dolly for a very dramatic affect.

Materials:
 1. Dolly that will stand upright
 2. Coveralls
 3. Paper/newspaper
 4. Clear tape
 5. Pair of gloves
 6. Small, American flag
 7. Large balloon
 8. Tin foil
 9. Cardboard box for oxygen tank
10. Roll of white paper
11. Small boxes for shoes
12. Colored markers
13. U.S. Space Camp T-Shirt patches
14. Solar blanket
15. Scissors

Coveralls:

Below are some web sites where you can purchase some inexpensive, disposable coveralls. You can also have the parents send money for you to purchase a coverall for each student and then you can attach the Space Camp patches to it and use a coverall instead of a T-Shirt for your student uniforms for the presentation.

1.

http://www.sciplus.com/   American Scientific Surplus

* Web site description – "Mess 'Em? Toss 'Em! Time for Junior to get his first taste of strained spinach! Lucky our zip-front, one-size-fits all disposable coveralls will fit someone over 6 ft tall, so Daddy can do the honors. (Shorter parents can pull up the elasticized legs and sleeves.) If Junior is 17, and hardly ever spits food at you anymore, the coveralls are perfect for painting, or crawling under the car or into the attic. Durable nonwoven material, one-piece including the hood. White only."
35351   **DISPOS COVERALL $2.95/EACH**

*****

2.

http://www.envirosafetyproducts.com/html/disposable coveralls. htm

Advantage Pro™   1 – 12 suits $3.50 each

*****

3.

http://www.safetyinfo.com/equipment/nextgen.htm

S412 Standard   Small to 2X $64.50 for 25 per case

*****

4.

http://www.toolprice.com/category/coveralls/

Disposable Coverall   Medium $1.79 each

*****

5.

http://www.uvprocess.com/products/Safety/Bodypro/DISPOSABLE COVERA
LLS.asp

DISPOSABLE COVERALLS

$9.00 EACH

Part Number I003-003   COVERALL:TYVEK SMALL

*****

Solar Blanket:

http://www.nitro-pak.com/product info.php/cPath/79 111/products
id/855?os Csid=7dde 1894bd9420a2ef3c30ac51d441ca

* **Web site description** – "Product Description Special SPACE
Edition - Gold/ Silver Space Blanket Summer Special $3.20

SPACE ®Brand EMERGENCY BLANKET is about the size of a package of
cigarettes, but opens to a 56" (142cm) by 84" (214cm) tough and
durable blanket. Manufactured by MPI since 1964 of the finest
polyester material and purest vacuum deposited aluminum for the
reflective surface, this product has helped to save countless
lives, by providing protection from the elements.

Used worldwide in disaster relief, rescue, and by militaries, this product is a 2 ounce life insurance policy. Will help prevent hypothermia by reflecting and retaining body heat, it is also very effective in preventing trauma shock, using the same reflective qualities. Available in silver/silver for regular use and Orange/Silver for greater visibility against a snow or water background. Registered FDA Medical Device No. 1220702. This is the ORIGINAL SPACE® BLANKET made exclusively in America, since 1964.

The SPACE® Brand blankets are used the world over by the Red Cross, Military Units, Medical Personnel, Search and Rescue Groups, and various Relief Agencies. They have been field proven since 1964 and have SAVED the LIVES of hundreds of people. Made of super insulating material. Super compact & light-weight; 2 oz. Opens to 56" x 84". USA Made. All-weather use. Can also be used as an emergency shelter, emergency snow visor (can be seen through), windbreak, sunshade protection (summer), radar reflector, or large signal mirror."

Chapter 12

Performance Sign

When my students and I were thinking of a name to call our presentation, I was thinking out loud and said **"Space, science and..."** One of my second graders immediately finished the title by saying, **"other things."** I loved it and the title has remained for the last eight years..."**Space, Science and Other Things.**"

With the orbiter and the Mission Control Board behind me on stage, I realized that my table with my supplies for the experiments looked rather stark and uninviting. I covered the front of the table with something that would tie in with the "WOW Factor" of the stage and the space shuttle. My students and I created a simple sign stating the title of the show and the name of our school.

We used a big box that we cut open and covered with construction paper. You can make the sign as large or as small as you like. I would always hide my boxes and any extra material that I needed (e.g., trash bag, balloons) for the show underneath the table for ready access. The sign will cover the mess and advertise your school's name.

We had fun making the words out of different colored construction paper. Again, be creative and come up with your own sign.

Materials:
1. Large piece of cardboard (5 ft. x 3 ft.)
2. Roll of white, construction paper
3. Various, colored, construction paper
4. Glue
5. Scissors
6. Stencils for making letters
7. Pen, marker/crayon, pencil for making letters

Make a sign without the school's name on it for the performances that you will do for other schools without your students. See below. Keep the sign so you don't have to keep making it for each performance.

Chapter 13

Music

Materials:
1. Sound track from "**Star Wars**"
2. Song – "**I've Got the Power**"
3. Song – "**Mission Control**"
4. CD/Cassette Player (Optional – piano)

♪ Sound Track from "Star Wars"

While the students are coming into the place where the presentation will be held, play the sound track from "Star Wars" on a cassette/CD player. This will help build the excitement of the show.

♪ "I've Got the Power" by Snap

During the first part of the show, the song will be used as dance music for audience volunteers. **See Chapter 1 – Show Manifest, page 1,** for complete details.

Purchase the CD/cassette of "I've Got the Power" by Snap. Edit the song by only taping the lyrics below to make a string of lyrics about five minutes long.

I've got the power hey yeah heh
I've got the power
Oh-oh-oh-oh-oh-oh-oh-oh-oh yeah-eah-eah-eah-eah-eah
I've got the power
Oh-oh-oh-oh-oh-oh-oh-oh-oh yeah-eah-eah-eah-eah-eah
Gettin' kinda heavy

It's gettin' it's gettin' it's gettin' kinda hectic
It's gettin' it's gettin' it's gettin' kinda hectic
It's gettin' it's gettin' it's gettin' kinda hectic
It's gettin' it's gettin' it's gettin' kinda hectic

I've got the power hey yeah heh
I've got the power
Oh-oh-oh-oh-oh-oh-oh-oh-oh yeah-eah-eah-eah-eah-eah
I've got the power
Oh-oh-oh-oh-oh-oh-oh-oh-oh yeah-eah-eah-eah-eah-eah
Gettin' kinda heavy.

Once the volunteers are on stage with you, tell them **"knowledge is power"** and play the recording for a few minutes. Tell the volunteers to start dancing. From this point you will go right into the magic trick, "I've got the Power" – D'Lite Magic Thumbs, where the audience will throw you the power. **See Chapter 2 – Teacher's Guide, page 19.** Play the same recording when the Aliens try to get the power. **See Chapter 2 – Teacher's Guide, page 48.**

"Mission Control" – Words and Music by Carmino Ravosa from the book World of Music, Silver Burdett & Ginn, 1991 (Scott Foresman)

At the end of the presentation (if you are using your students) the Commander will say, **"Attention! Line up!"** When everyone is in line across the center of the stage, the Commander will say, **"At ease!"** The students will sing along with the cassette if you were able to find it (or have someone play the piano). You or a volunteer will start the music. Have your students perform any special hand or eye movements that you like while they are singing (e.g., When they sing about Venus or Mars, have them point up to the sky). At the end of the song, the students will salute the audience and bow. **See Chapter 2 – Teacher's Guide, page 69.**

The Department of Defense Schools uses the song in their second grade music book called Music for Living, World of Music, by Silver Burdett & Ginn, 1991 (Scott Foresman). Audiotapes are also supplied with the book. Check with **www.google.com** as to where you can obtain/purchase a copy of the tape. I purchased a copy of the book on **www.ebay.com**.

Spaced Travel
http://www.edu-cyberpg.com/Music/spacetravel.html

Mission Control
Words and music by Carmino Ravosa

Mission Control do you read me?
Will you please save me a place?
Mission Control do you need me
On the next rocket in space?

Vs. 1

Maybe I'm small but I'm growing.
Watch and one day you will see.
Space is wide open and waiting for me.

REFRAIN
So, Mission Control do you read me?
I really don't take too much room.
Mission Control do you need me
On the next trip to the moon.

Vs. 2

I want to study the planets.
I want to study the stars.
I want to go up to Venus or Mars.

REFRAIN

Vs. 3

I'm working hard and I'm certain
An astronaut's what I will be.
The sky is the limit for someone like me.

REFRAIN

(Spoken) Mission Control, do you read me?
I'll be seeing you in about twenty years.
Until then, over and out.

For more of Mr. Carmino Ravosa's music, please see the books The World of Music and The Music Connection by Silver Burdett & Ginn, 1991, (Scott Foresman).
Mr. Ravosa can be contacted at carminoravosa@yahoo.com for your future musical needs.

With permission from Mr.Carmino Ravosa:

Space is wide o - pen and wait-ing for me. _____

So, Mis-sion Con-trol, __ do you read me?

I real-ly don't take __ too much room.

Mis-sion Con-trol, __ do you need me

Last time, to Ending

On the next trip to the moon?

2. I want to study the planets.
    I want to study the stars.
    I want to go up to Venus, or Mars.
    So, Mission Control . . .

3. I'm working hard, and I'm certain
    An astronaut's what I will be.
    The sky is the limit for someone like me.
    So, Mission Control . . .

Ending (spoken):
    Mission Control, do you read me?
    I'll be seeing you in about twenty years.
    Until then, over and out.

Links for Space Songs:

1. **Singing Science Records**
http://www.acme.com/jef/science_songs/

2. **The Science Series: Space**
http://www.amazon.com/exec/obidos/tg/detail/-/B00000JYGK/102-1842909-6064955?v=glance

3. **Dr. Chocolate Sings**
http://www.tranquility.net/~scimusic/

4. **"Adventures in Space"** song by Greg & Steve to act out being astronauts ***Note** - This is a great song to finish the show. The smaller children love it since the song requires them to get out of their seats and move around acting as if they were in space. You will need a large area for them to move.
http://www.allegro-music.com/gregsteve.asp

5. **"MusicSpace"** celebrates music that is written for space exploration. Or is about space exploration. Or is played in space. Or makes you feel like you are in space. Or is actually from space.
http://www.hobbyspace.com/Music/index.html#NASAMusic

6. **"ABC for Kids** - Songs of From Outer Space"
http://shop.abc.net.au/browse/product.asp?productid=327394

Links for Space Activities:

1. Gigglepotz
http://www.gigglepotz.com/science.htm

2. Marianne Dyson's Space Science Activities
http://www.mariannedyson.com/spaceactivities.html

3. Deep Space Network
http://deepspace.jpl.nasa.gov/dsn/educ/children.html

4. DLTK's Crafts for Kids Outer Space Section
http://www.dltk-kids.com/crafts/space/space.html
*Note - Wonderful site for space activities for the classroom.

Chapter 14

Orbiter Experiments

This chapter includes two experiments you can do with your students in your classroom. Inflate the orbiter in your room and let your student practice a mock space mission. ***Note** – The original experiments were given to me at a Science Teacher's Conference in North Carolina in 1996. There was no author's credit information on the papers. The experiments have been re-written and adapted for my classroom use.

36	10	19	7	21	4
13	26	1	3	16	27
9	23	18	32	25	35
17	28	12	31	6	14
5	33	24	29	22	30
11	15	8	20	34	2

Experiment # 1 – Number Grid

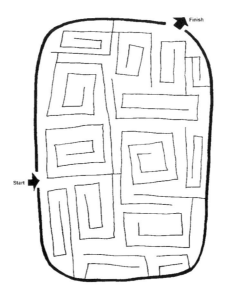

Experiment # 2 – Maze

Experiment # 1 – Number Grid

Problem: Can microgravity-induced disorientation affect an astronaut's eye-hand response time?

Materials:
1. Grid with 36 squares numbered randomly from 1-36
2. Stopwatch
3. Pencils
4. Swivel chair

Procedure:
1. Outside of the orbiter prior to launch, have one astronaut place his/her finger on number 1 and say the number, one.
2. Repeat step #1 for each successive number up to the number 15.
3. Record how many seconds it takes for each astronaut to identify and locate all 15 numbers.
4. Repeat step #3, two more times and find the average.
5. Inside of the orbiter, at the appointed time during the mission, select one astronaut and spin him/her around 10 times in a swivel chair.
6. After the astronaut is finished spinning in the swivel chair, repeat steps #1 – 4.
7. Report results to Mission Control

Data:

Name _____

Time on the ground outside of orbiter
      1st _____
      2nd _____
      3rd _____
Average _____

Time in shuttle
      1st _____
      2nd _____
      3rd _____
Average _____

Experiment # 1 - Number Grid

36	10	19	7	21	4
13	26	1	3	16	27
9	23	18	32	25	35
17	28	12	31	6	14
5	33	24	29	22	30
11	15	8	20	34	2

Experiment # 2 - Maze

Problem: Can microgravity-induced disorientation affect an astronaut's eye-hand response time?

Materials:
1. Copy of worksheet - Experiment #2 - Maze
2. Stopwatch
3. Pencils
4. Swivel chair

Procedure:
1. Outside of the orbiter prior to launch, have one astronaut place pencil on the word, "start."
2. Record how many seconds it takes for each astronaut to complete the maze.
3. Repeat step #2, two more times and find the average.
4. Inside of the orbiter at the appointed time during the mission, select one astronaut and spin him/her around 10 times in a swivel chair.
5. After the astronaut is finished spinning in the swivel chair, repeat steps #1 - 3.
6. Report results to Mission Control.

Data:

Name _____

Time on the ground outside of orbiter
       1st _____
       2nd _____
       3rd _____
Average _____

Time in shuttle
       1st _____
       2nd _____
       3rd _____
Average _____

Experiment # 2 – Maze

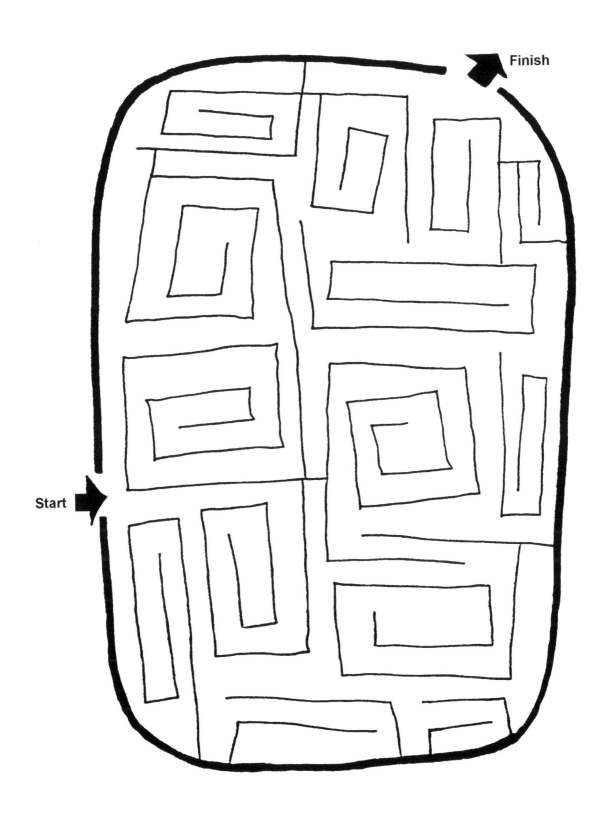

Chapter 15

Mini Space Shuttle Instructions

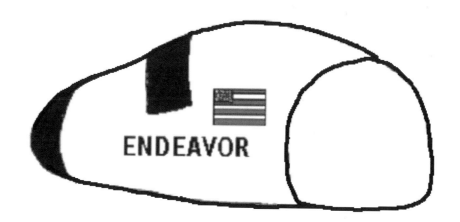

       This would be a good activity to do with your classroom students or other teachers to help them understand the cuts and angles needed to construct the larger space shuttle cabin.

       These directions have been created for a "trash bag" version for students to make a mini shuttle at their desks. The directions incorporate reading, science, art and math skills to complete the project.

       If you do the smaller version of the space shuttle first, constructing the larger shuttle will be much easier for you.

Materials:
1. Two, white, trash bags
2. Scissors
3. Ruler
4. Clear, white tape
5. Black, trash bag
6. Construction paper (red, white and blue)
7. Straight edge
8. Paper for stuffing
9. Erasable, overhead markers

White Trash Bag:
1. Cut the bottom seam off of a large, white trash bag. Also, cut the top of the bag if there is some kind of seam or threading on it.
2. Cut one of the side seams open and spread the trash bag open.

3. Measure down 12 inches from the top of the bag and using a straight edge draw a straight line with an erasable, overhead projector marker.

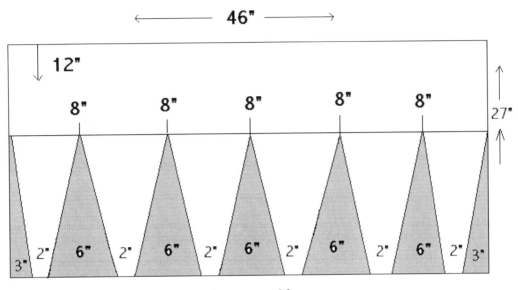

Diagram 41

4. Starting at the edge of the bag, measure every 8 inches and mark the spot on the line.
5. Along the bottom of the bag, measure over 3 inches and mark that spot.
6. Starting from the 3 inch mark, measure over 2 inches and mark that spot.
7. Starting from the 2 inch mark, measure over 6 inches and mark that spot.
8. Continue marking the bag every 2 inches and every 6 inches until you come to the end of the bag where you should have 3 inches left (approximately).
9. Following the pattern in the diagram below and using an erasable, overhead projector marker, draw lines from the 8 inch mark on the top line to the 2 inch and 6 inch marks on the bottom of the bag.
10. Draw lines to form triangles.
11. Cut out the 6 inch and 3 inches pieces of the bag. Cut out the shaded pieces of Diagram 41.
12. Overlapping the edges slightly, tape the edges together and trim the excess.
13. Tape the side seam. **See Diagram 42.**

White Trash Bag

Diagram 42

14. Using a black trash bag, cut out a 6 inch diameter black circle. **See Diagram 43.**

Diagram 43

15. Tape the black circle to the nose cone of the cabin. It won't fit perfectly, so make it fit. **See Diagram 44.**

Diagram 44

16. Turn the trash bag inside out.
17. Cut a 16 inch diameter white circle out of another trash bag. **See Diagram 45.**

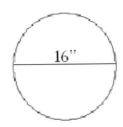

Diagram 45

18. Tape the white circle to the back of the shuttle cabin leaving a six-inch hole open. **See Diagram 46.**

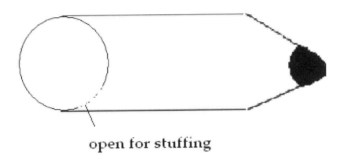

open for stuffing

Diagram 46

19. Fill the shuttle with crushed paper to give the shuttle form.
20. After filling the shuttle with paper to the wanted shape, tape the six-inch hole closed.
21. Decorate the orbiter with construction paper. Tape the decorations onto the shuttle using clear tape.

Further Additions:

To make a complete shuttle, tape a shoebox covered with white paper to the orbiter cabin for the cargo bay area. Attach cardboard wings and another small box for the fuselage. Let your students be creative and build/decorate the rest of the shuttle using various household products.

Chapter 16

Letters, Permission Form, Certificates

This chapter is designed to give you some ideas for creating letters to parents, permission forms and awards for your students participating in the space production. The actual letters, awards and permission forms will follow the descriptions. The certificates are located in **Appendix C (pages 218 - 225)**.

Letters:

Letter #1

Space Show

Dear Parents, Guardians, Visitors,

Date _____

_____
Teacher   Grade

_____
School

will be presenting a "Chemistry/Physics -

Interactive Space Show" at _____

On _____ time _____ .

    Explosions, sparks of electricity and fire will fill the room as part of a live show that will illustrate the effects of science on the real world while captivating the audience.
    The presentation will be approximately 1½ hours. There will be experiments on density, air pressure, vacuums, amplification of sound, static electricity, and combustion science mixed with magic tricks and music using a space theme along with a ½ scale model version of the Endeavor orbiter cabin. The students will perform a mock landing of the Endeavor Play.
    Fifty-five audience volunteers will be needed to demonstrate scientific principals. Please attend our presentation and be sure to watch for mystery guests (visitors).
    For further information please contact:

_____
Name   Phone

Letter #1 - <u>Parents, Guardians, Visitors - Presentation Information Letter</u> to inform people of the date, place, and time of your production. The letter will give the parents, guests, and visitors, a small synopsis of the production.

Space Show

Date _____

Dear Parents, Guardians, Visitors,

_____
Teacher   Grade

_____
School

will be presenting a "Chemistry/Physics –

Interactive Space Show" at _____

on _____ time _____ .

Explosions, sparks of electricity and fire will fill the room as part of a live show that will illustrate the effects of science on the real world while captivating the audience.

The presentation will be approximately 1½ hours. There will be experiments on density, air pressure, vacuums, amplification of sound, static electricity, and combustion…science mixed with magic tricks and music using a space theme along with a ½ scale model version of the Endeavor orbiter cabin. The students will perform a mock landing of the *Endeavor Landing Play*.

Fifty-five audience volunteers will be needed to demonstrate scientific principals. Please attend our presentation and be sure to watch for mystery guests (visitors).

For further information please contact:

_____
Name   Phone

Letter #2

Space Show

SPACE, SCIENCE
AND
OTHER THINGS

Date _____

Dear Parents/Guardians,

_____ will be presenting a Chemistry/Physics

Space Show, on _____ at _____ .

The presentation will be approximately 1½ hours. There will be experiments on density, air pressure, vacuums, amplification of sound, static electricity, and combustion – science mixed with magic tricks and music using a space theme along with a ½ scale model version of the Endeavor orbiter cabin. The students will perform a mock landing of the Endeavor Play.

Our class is extremely excited about the upcoming space presentation for our school.

*Your child will need to bring a solid white T-shirt for his/her part in the presentation. Please send the shirt to school no later than _____ .

Space Camp uniform T-shirts will be made using taped-on patches. The tape can easily be removed and will not damage the shirt.

If any parent would like to help out on the days of the presentation, I would be very grateful. Help will be needed in setting up the stage and cleaning up after the presentation. Two parents/volunteers will also be needed to help on stage with the Van de Graff Generator and help with the Endeavor Landing Play.

If you are willing to volunteer, please send a white T-shirt for yourself, so you can also be in uniform while on stage and be part of our production.

Yours in education,

Letter #2 – Parents/Guardians – Help Letter requesting T-Shirts for students and volunteers for help with the production.

Space Show

SPACE, SCIENCE
AND
OTHER THINGS

Date _____

Dear Parents/Guardians,

_____ will be presenting a Chemistry/Physics

Space Show, on _____ at _____ .

The presentation will be approximately 1½ hours. There will be experiments on density, air pressure, vacuums, amplification of sound, static electricity, and combustion - science mixed with magic tricks and music using a space theme along with a ½ scale model version of the Endeavor orbiter cabin. The students will perform a mock landing of the Endeavor Play.

Our class is extremely excited about the upcoming space presentation for our school.

Your child will need to bring a solid white T-Shirt for his/her part in the presentation. Please send the shirt to school no later than _____ .

Space Camp uniform T-Shirts will be made using taped-on patches. The tape can easily be removed and will not damage the shirt.

If any parent would like to help out on the days of the presentation, I would be very grateful. Help will be needed in setting up the stage and cleaning up after the presentation. Two parents/volunteers will also be needed to help on stage with the Van de Graff Generator and help with the *Endeavor Landing Play*.

If you are willing to volunteer, please send a white T-Shirt for yourself, so you can also be in uniform while on stage and be part of our production.

Yours in education,

_____

Permission Form:

SPACE, SCIENCE
AND
OTHER THINGS

Space Show

Date_____

SPACE, SCIENCE & OTHER THINGS
FIELD TRIP PERMISSION FORM

On _____ the _____ grade class will
present "Space, Science, & Other Things" - the Chemistry/
Physics Interactive Space Show to the student body

at _____ .

My child _____

_____ **has** _____ **does not have** my permission to attend the
presentation.

Teacher _____ Grade _____ Room# _____

SPACE, SCIENCE
AND
OTHER THINGS

Space Show

Date_____

SPACE, SCIENCE & OTHER THINGS
FIELD TRIP PERMISSION FORM

On _____ the _____ grade class will
present "Space, Science, & Other Things" - the Chemistry/
Physics Interactive Space Show to the student body

at _____ .

My child _____

_____ **has** _____ **does not have** my permission to attend the
presentation.

Teacher _____ Grade _____ Room# _____

Field Trip Permission Form - use if the presentation is held off
the school campus in a theater or another large area. To save
paper, there are two permission slips per page.

Space Show

SPACE, SCIENCE
AND
OTHER THINGS

Date_____

SPACE, SCIENCE & OTHER THINGS
FIELD TRIP PERMISSION FORM

On _____ the _____ grade class will present "Space, Science, & Other Things" - the Chemistry/Physics Interactive Space Show to the student body

at _____.

My child _____

_____ **has** _____ **does not have** my permission to attend the presentation.

Teacher _____ Grade _____ Room# _____

Space Show

SPACE, SCIENCE
AND
OTHER THINGS

Date_____

SPACE, SCIENCE & OTHER THINGS
FIELD TRIP PERMISSION FORM

On _____ the _____ grade class will present "Space, Science, & Other Things" - the Chemistry/Physics Interactive Space Show to the student body

at _____.

My child _____

_____ **has** _____ **does not have** my permission to attend the presentation.

Teacher _____ Grade _____ Room# _____

CERTIFICATES:

Scan the pictures of my previous certificates to use for your needs or create your own forms. Please see **Appendix C (pages 218 – 225)**.

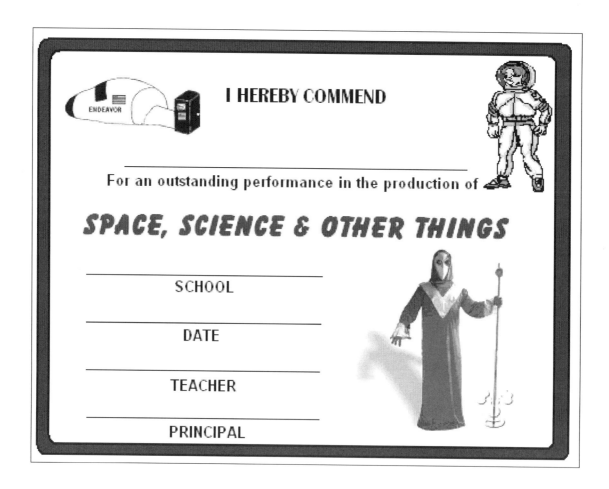

Chapter 17

Vocabulary Words

Listed below are vocabulary words for your students from the presentation.

1. Have your students look up the definition of the words.
2. Have your students use the words in a sentence.
3. Have your students make new words from the letters of the vocabulary word (e.g., chemical change - me, I, can, him, ale, chain, lane, high, etc.)
4. Have your students put the words on index cards, mix them up and put them in alphabetical order.
5. Have your students make compound words out of some of the vocabulary words by combining them with other ordinary words (e.g., balance - balance beam; base - baseball; atom - atom bomb; oxygen - oxygen mask)

Air	Acid
Air Pressure	Alien
Astronaut	Atom
Balance	Base
Carbon Dioxide	Centrifugal Force
Change	Chemical
Chemical Change	Circuit
Closed Circuit	Contracting
Expanding	Electricity
Electron	Element
Expanding	Experiment
Explode	Forces
Gas	High Pressure

Hoberman Sphere	Hydrogen
Hypothesis	Implode
Inertia	Knowledge
Launcher	Laws of Motion
Low Pressure	Matter
Molecule	Nature
Negative	Neutron
Neutral	Open Circuit
Orbiter	Oxygen
Physical Change	Positive Power
Pressure	Proton
Reaction	Rocket
Science	Shuttle
Sound Vibrations	Sound Waves
Sphere	Telekinesis
Thrust	Variable
Van de Graaf Generator	

Come up with your own words from the presentation.

Chapter 18

Curriculum Standards and Objectives

Listed below are the Science Curriculum Standards and Objectives from the Department of Defense Education Activity (DoDEA) PreK-6[h] Grade - Science web site that could be applied to the space presentation. Some of the "examples" have been slightly modified to fit the objectives for the space show. Use as many as you need or use them as examples for creating your own objectives for the production.

*Web site description - "To create a world-class education system, DoDEA has developed rigorous and demanding curriculum standards. The curriculum standards specify what students should know and be able to do. DoDEA curriculum standards are based on the content standards produced by the National Council of Teachers of Mathematics, the National Council of Teachers of English/the International Reading Association, the National Research Council's National Science Education Standards and the National Council for Teachers of Social Studies.

Standards are important because they set high levels of learning and performance for all students. The standards also serve as a basis for assessment across the curriculum. They focus on what is important in each curriculum area."

http://www.dodea.edu/curriculum/

Prekindergarten
http://www.dodea.edu/curriculum/prekindergarten/science.htm

Inquiry Skills - Children learn to use inquiry skills to investigate their physical and natural world.

> **Objective** - Young children ask hundreds of questions to learn about their world. As a parent, you will want to prepare your child for a global world that constantly changes with new technology.

- **Explore the natural and physical world through observations** (e.g., observe physical changes such as water becoming steam)
- **Use tools to observe and report changes in his world** (e.g., use wind air bags and then draw pictures of observations)
- **Ask questions about changes in his/her world**

Physical Science - Children learn about physical properties of the world by observing and manipulating objects and materials within the environment.

Objective - Children will learn about the physical properties of the world through a variety of activities using blocks, dramatic play, sand and water, toys, art, woodworking, and outdoor play. It is important to use open-ended questions with a child this age (e.g., "I wonder why this big toy boat floats but the penny sinks?") to encourage investigation and problem-solving skills. As you interact with your child, describe physical changes in the natural environment as they occur.

- **Identify characteristics of objects** (e.g., size, shape, and texture)
- **Identify similarities and differences in objects** (e.g., observe the physical changes and chemical changes to a variety of substances)
- **Explore the position and motion of objects** (e.g., balloon race – motion of escaping air)

Earth and Space Science - Children learn about the earth and the sky.

Objective - Children will observe objects in the sky, and describe changes in the earth and sky by making observations, asking questions, and drawing conclusions. They will learn about the world by talking about the weather, rocks, water, and soil.

- **Explore properties of water and soil** (e.g., changing a liquid to a gas and imploding a can using a vacuum)
- **Observe changes in the physical environment** (e.g., watching the orbiter inflate with the use of air)

Science and Technology - Children learn to identify tools and technologies.

Objective - Children will investigate the ways science uses tools and technologies to help people work and solve problems.

- **Design and build structures from sand, blocks and other materials** (e.g., building a water fountain out of a bottle, balloon, water, clay, and a straw)
- **Identify technological tools and how they help with specific work** (e.g., space shuttle telephone to carry sound waves)

Science in Personal and Social Perspective - Children learn about safety and how to conserve resources.

Objective - Children will learn about personal and school safety. They will learn how to conserve resources in the classroom and ways to improve their environment.

- **Identify safety rules at school and home**
  Observe changes in his/her home and school environment

- **Practice ways to improve the environment** (e.g., cleaning up mess after experiments)

History and Nature of Science - Children learn that science is a human effort.

Objective - Children will identify how parents and neighbors use science and technology in their work.

- **Recognize that different jobs use science and technology in different ways** (e.g., air pressure can move things easier)

Kindergarten

http://www.dodea.edu/curriculum/kindergarten/science.htm

Inquiry Skills - Children learn to investigate the world around them by using the processes of scientific inquiry.

Objective - Children are naturally curious and will want to explore their world. Their questions can become the basis for conducting simple investigations.

- **Ask questions about his/her world**
- **Use tools to make observations** (e.g., use wind air bags and then draw pictures of observations; Van de Graaf generator to make static electricity and to make a fluorescent tube emit light)
- **Summarize and share what he/she has observed** (e.g., have he/she draw pictures to describe what he/she observed at the space presentation)

Physical Science - Children investigate the properties of objects and materials.

Objective - Children will notice that the natural world continually changes, and they will learn the vocabulary to describe these changes.

- **Use his/her senses** (e.g., touch, hearing) to identify objects
- **Describe objects using physical characteristics such as size, shape, color, and texture**
- **Use descriptive words to explain the movement of   objects in relationship to their surroundings** (e.g., fast and slow)

Earth and Space Science - Children identify the properties of Earth's materials.

Objective - Children wonder about such things as why the sky is blue, why things fall to the ground, where mountains come from, and how far away stars are in the night sky. They will explore the physical world around them and how it changes over time.

- **Explore properties of Earth's Materials: such as water and soil** (e.g., changing a liquid to a gas and imploding a can using a vacuum)

Science and Technology - Children identify simple tools of technology and how to use them in their daily lives.

> **Objective** - Children will be interested in the ways that technology affects their lives, such as how buildings are built and how computers work.

- **Identify technological tools**
- **Tell how technological tools can help people do work and solve problems.** (e.g., space shuttle telephone to carry sound waves)
- **Design and build structures using blocks, sand, and other materials** (e.g., building a water fountain out of a bottle, balloon, water, clay, and a straw)

History and Nature of Science - Children learn that science is a human effort.

> **Objective** - Children will explore how science and technology are used in daily life.

- **Identify ways that parents and neighbors use science and technology every day** (e.g., air pressure can move things easier; telephone uses for communication)

Grade One

http://www.dodea.edu/curriculum/1stGrade/science.htm

Inquiry skills - Students conduct investigations using inquiry skills.

> **Objective** - Every day is filled with opportunities to learn science. Students will explore their world by learning the steps of a simple experiment that leads to scientific explanations. They will use scientific words to summarize and explain their discoveries.

- **Use reliable sources for gathering information in investigations** (e.g., books or educational Web sites)
- **Tell how to plan and conduct a simple investigation to solve a problem or answer a question** (e.g., acids and bases experiments)
- **Ask questions or make predictions using scientific Words** (e.g., make hypothesis about how many breaths of air it would take to fill one air bag)
- **Use scientific words when discussing or summarizing the results of the investigation** (e.g., balloon race: variables, wind bag, hypothesis)
- **Organize information and find ways to tell others about his investigation** (e.g., follow-up suggestion – drawing pictures of investigation)

Physical Science - Students explore the characteristics of objects, light, motion, heat, and magnetism.

> **Objective** - Students will conduct hands-on investigations where they can see, touch, manipulate, and modify Materials: to explore the characteristics of light, motion, heat, and magnetism.

- **Use standard units of measurement in weighing and measuring objects** (e.g., grams, liters, meters; ounces, pounds, feet – acid and base experiments)
- **Identify two states of water** (i.e., liquid versus steam in can experiment)
- **Explore the motion of an object through speed, position, and direction** (e.g., balloon race)
- **Identify that movement has different speeds** (e.g., slow and fast – balloon race)
- **Investigate sources of light and heat** (e.g. fire experiments)

Science and Technology - Students examine simple technology tools.

> **Objective** - Students will recognize simple technological tools and how these tools assist them in their classroom and home settings. Using information on how technology supports people, students will develop a simple plan to demonstrate their understanding of a technological tool.

- **Identify technological uses and how they can help at home and school** (e.g., a computer, a telephone, a VCR)

Science in Personal and Social Perspectives - Students demonstrate an understanding of science in relationship to self and society.

> **Objective** - Students will practice safety when conducting scientific investigations, describe changes and characteristics in a population, identify types of resources, and describe how environments change.

- **Practice safety when conducting science activities** (e.g., not taste anything unless he/she is sure it's okay to eat and it's sanitary, wear rubber gloves when handling certain items, wear goggles if something could endanger his/her eyes, minimize the risk of accidents by following certain steps and procedures, follow warnings on labels and instructions, and ask for help from an adult if he/she isn't sure about something or an accident occurs)

History and Nature of Science - Students identify science as a human effort.

> **Objective** - Students will understand how scientific investigations are used to explore the world within the school and community settings.

- **Identify science investigations within the classroom setting**

Grade Two

http://www.dodea.edu/curriculum/2ndGrade/science.htm

Inquiry Skills - Students conduct investigations using the processes of scientific inquiry.

> **Objective** - Students will use a broad range of inquiry skills to understand their natural world. They will learn to make more detailed observations and conclusions, and use unusual or unexpected data to help them validate information.

- **Gather scientific information from a variety of reliable sources**
- **Design and conduct investigations**
- **Ask questions about the data that has been collected, and then report his/her observations and predictions using scientific words. Learn to use graphs to explain scientific information Build models to explain scientific learning** (e.g., build a slinky telephone)
- **Describe procedures and results of his/her observations and investigations orally and in writing**
- **Summarize the data, and state a conclusion orally and in writing**

Physical Science - Students identify the properties of objects and materials.

> **Objective** - Students will learn about the different states of matter and how to classify objects according to their physical characteristics. Their knowledge of the physical world will be gained through investigations with rocks and soil, and through activities with light and magnetism.

- **Conduct experiments that demonstrate the three states of matter**
- **Develop classification systems to sort objects based on physical characteristics**
- **Explore motion of objects by moving objects of different sizes and weights**
- **Record and describe the directional paths of objects** (e.g., circular, straight, zigzag, high/low)
- **Explore ways to produce different speeds to produce different sounds** (e.g., a fan on low, medium, and high speeds)
- **Compare techniques and forces needed for moving objects**

Science and Technology - Students identify simple technologies and demonstrate inquiry abilities in technology design.

> **Objective** - Students will explore how simple technological tools assist them in classroom and home settings. Using the information on how technology supports people, students will identify a problem in their immediate environment and then propose and implement a solution.

- Identify a problem in his/her immediate environment (e.g., magic paper - Why did it completely burn)
- Communicate methods and solutions orally, in writing, or in pictures

Science in Personal and Social Perspectives - Students practice safety in science activities, practice conservation of resources, and understand how humans interact with the environment.

> Objective - Students will practice safety when conducting scientific investigations. They will describe changes and characteristics in a population, identify types of resources, and describe how environments change.

- Practice safety when he/she is involved in scientific activities

Grade Three

http://www.dodea.edu/curriculum/3rdGrade/

Inquiry Skills - Students conduct investigations using inquiry skills.

> Objective - Students will learn to develop questions, form simple hypotheses (unproved theories), make predictions, and gather data. Students will use this data to make deductions and develop conclusions.

- Use information from a variety of reliable sources (e.g., library books, educational web sites, and textbooks)
- Design and conduct experiments to test scientific hypotheses (unproved assumptions)
- Ask questions, make predictions and develop explanations about data (e.g., encourage him/her to explore the natural world through observations. Talk with him/her about his/her discoveries and have him/her make predictions or give explanations based on what he/she has observed.)
- Use scientific words (e.g. variables, hypothesis, expanding, contracting, chemical reaction)
- Organize and analyze information he/she has collected and report on it through graphs, orally, or in writing
  Summarize and state a conclusion regarding the investigation

Physical Science - Students identify the properties of objects and materials.

> Objective - Students will explore how energy and force interact with matter.

- Investigate ways to change the motion of objects (e.g., on a nature walk, ask him/her to observe how the wind moves objects such as tree branches, coke cans, feathers, and paper)

- **Arrive at the conclusion that objects moving faster will travel further in a given time** (e.g. balloon race)
- **Investigate how changes in force cause changes in motion** (e.g., ask him/her what happens when a person with more weight and force-such as an adult-kicks a soccer ball or throws a softball)

Science and Technology - Students investigate different technologies.

> **Objective** - Students will identify technological tools and their purpose. Using the information on how technology supports people, students will identify a problem in the immediate environment and propose, implement, and evaluate a possible solution.

- **Examine unfamiliar tools and guess how they are used**
- **Identify a problem in the immediate environment and propose possible solutions** (e.g., acid & base experiments)
- **Implement proposed solutions and evaluate the results** (e.g., acid & base experiments)

History and Nature of Science - Students learn that science is a human effort.

> **Objective** - Students will recognize the contributions of discoveries and inventions in peoples' lives. They will recognize they can use science process skills in the classroom setting.

- **Recognize that science is an activity that he/she can do in the classroom and at home** (Encourage him/her to use scientific process skills in his/her everyday life activities. Scientific process skills include using your senses to gather information about the environment, looking for commonalties and differences in grouping objects or events, using measurement to make estimates or record data, basing conclusions on facts and observations, and predicting what will happen next in an investigation.)

Grade Four
http://www.dodea.edu/curriculum/4thGrade/

Inquiry Skills - Students conduct investigations using inquiry skills.

> **Objective** - Students will observe and collect data, and analyze experimental results. They will use no more than two variables in their investigations and make simple predictions using picture, bar, and line graphs. At this level the student's ability to question and hypothesize (predict) is more detailed and specific.

- **Use information from a variety of reliable sources** (e.g., library books, educational web sites, and textbooks)
- **Design and conduct experiments to test scientific hypotheses** (unproved assumptions) (e.g., test the hypothesis)

- Select appropriate tools to collect and record data (e.g., to chart daily temperature, use a thermometer)
- Ask questions, make predictions, and develop explanations about data
- Use scientific words (e.g. variables, hypothesis, expanding, contracting, chemical reaction)
- Organize and analyze information he/she has collected and report on it through graphs, orally, or in writing
- Summarize and state a conclusion regarding the investigation

Physical Science - Students identify the properties of objects and materials.

Objective - Students will examine and classify matter and its properties. Students will investigate the changes in matter under certain conditions.

- Investigate ways to change the motion of objects
- Arrive at the conclusion that objects moving faster will travel further in a given time
- Investigate how changes in force cause changes in motion

Science and Technology - Students investigate different technologies.

Objective - Students will explore technological tools that are used to collect data, make and organize observations, analyze results, and accomplish tasks effectively.

- Examine unfamiliar tools and guess how they are used
- Identify the materials used in creating a variety of objects
- Identify a problem in the immediate environment and propose possible solutions
- Implement proposed solutions and evaluate the results (e.g., obtain data, record it on paper, and then analyze the information collected)
- Communicate methods and solutions orally, in writing, and through pictures and graphs (Explore the use of a computer to draw and write solutions.)

Science in Personal and Social Perspectives - Students practice safety in science activities, practice conservation of resources, and understand how humans interact with the environment.

Objective - Students will practice safety when conducting scientific investigations. They will describe the many changes, both natural and manufactured, that affect the quality of life on Earth.

- Demonstrate personal and group safety when participating in science activities at home (e.g., help him/her develop a respect for safety by understanding what is safe and unsafe behavior when conducting science investigations, whether at home or school)

History and Nature of Science - Students learn that science is a human effort.

> **Objective** - Students will compare science and technology of the past with science and technology of today. They will learn about scientists of various backgrounds.

- **Recognize that science is an activity that he/she can do in the classroom and at home** (Encourage him to use scientific process skills in his/her everyday life activities. Scientific process skills include using your senses to gather information about the environment, looking for commonalties and differences in grouping objects or events, using measurement to make estimates or record data, basing conclusions on facts and observations, and predicting what will happen next in an investigation.)
- **Identify men and women from different cultures who have contributed to science and technology**

Grade Five

http://www.dodea.edu/curriculum/5thGrade/

Inquiry Skills - Students conduct investigations using inquiry skills.

> **Objective** - Students will learn to think scientifically by using all of their senses or scientific investigations to answer questions about their world. Students will collect and analyze data and verify experimental results. They will define the variables in the investigation and make simple predictions using picture, bar, and line graphs. They will use scientific words to describe and report their findings.

- **Evaluate information from a variety of reliable sources** (For example, books, Web sites, scientific magazines, articles)
- **Design and conduct observational and experimental investigations** (For example, encourage your child to ask new questions and use all the senses-sight, hearing, smell, taste, and touch-when processing scientific information in daily life.)
- **Select and use appropriate tools to collect and record information from observations and experiments** (For example, ask a question such as "How does a car's shape affect its speed?" and have your child tell you the tools and methods he/she would use to test possible answers.)
- **Use classification in the inquiry process** (for example, size, shape, and color)
- **Organize and explain the information collected in scientific investigations** (For example, sequential steps, a cause-and-effect chart, or a Venn diagram, two circles over-lapping in the middle, to organize and process science information)
- **Use scientific words in explanations**

- **Analyze, interpret, and evaluate information obtained from observations and/or experiments** (For example, encourage your child to break down the information into organized chunks to aid in understanding.)
- **Describe his/her observations and/or experiments, including procedures and results, orally and in writing**
- **Summarize the data of his or her observations and/or experiments and state conclusions**

Physical Science - Students compare properties and changes in properties and understand how energy is transferred.

Objective - Students will describe matter and energy by its properties and changes. They will investigate the physical and chemical changes in matter, as well as the processes that change the form of energy.

- **Define matter as anything that has mass, takes up space, and occurs in solid, liquid, or gas form**
- **Describe the changes to matter when heat is added or taken away** (For example, a marshmallow that is toasted or sugar that is heated)
- **Explain the concepts of mass** (a measure of how much matter there is in an object) **and volume** (the amount of space an object occupies)
- **Conduct investigations of matter to compare physical properties (such as color, texture, and odor) and chemical properties** (For example, iron becoming rusty when exposed to air)
- **Tell what happens when matter becomes a new substance** (For example, describe the processes of changing ice to liquid water and then to gas vapor.)
- **Explore ways that energy is transferred** (For example, radiation, conduction, and convection)
- **Describe and demonstrate the characteristics of sound waves** (For example, a wavelength is the distance from one air compression to another; frequency is the number of complete waves produced in a unit of time; and amplitude is the measure of the amount of energy in a sound.)
- **Provide examples of how different forms of energy are used in everyday applications** (For example, light bulbs, heat from the sun, TV, and radio broadcasts)

Earth and Space Science - Students explore the properties and changes in Earth's land and sky.

Objective - Students will use a model of Earth to understand its composition and structure, including the study of factors that influence its geologic history. They will investigate the characteristics of planets and stars and study patterns involving Earth in the solar system.

- **Explain how the celestial bodies in the solar system move in predictable patterns** (For example, take a family outing to a local planetarium or explore comets, meteorites, and micrometeorites on NASA's Web site: **http://kids.msfc.nasa.gov/news/2002/news-mystery.asp**. The site has photos, explanations, and activities for students.)

Science and Technology - Students identify technologies and demonstrate abilities in technology design.

Objective - Students will use technology to create a technological design. Students explore the benefits and consequences of technology in their environment.

- **Design a solution for an identified problem using a technological design** (For example, discuss some possible inventions that would be needed to survive on the moon.)
- **Determine criteria that would be used to gauge the success of the solution**
- **Evaluate the completed solution and determine ways to improve the design**
- **Illustrate that technology is constantly changing** (For example, discuss how the size and capacity of computers has changed over the past 10-15 years.)

Science in Personal and Social Perspectives - Students demonstrate safety in science.

Objective - Students will practice safety in science activities; understand the interrelationships of populations, resources, and environments; and examine risks and benefits of personal and social decisions.

- **Demonstrate personal safety in science activities at home and school**

History of Science - Students understand that science is a human effort.

Objective - Students will explore the history of science and how scientists through time have used new evidence to make changes to theories and accepted ideas.

- **Identify scientists, both men and women, of various ethnic backgrounds**
- **Describe how scientists in the past have broken through the accepted ideas of their time to reach conclusions that we currently take for granted** (For example, together read about Galileo and his discoveries.)

Grade Six

http://www.dodea.edu/curriculum/6thGrade/

Inquiry Skills - Students plan and conduct scientific investigations using inquiry skills.

Objective - Students will collect and analyze data, and verify experimental results. They will define the variables in the experiment and make simple predictions using picture, bar, and line graphs. They will use scientific words to describe and report observations and experiments.

- **Identify questions that he or she can answer through scientific investigations** (For example, help your child develop the attitude that taking a scientific approach is like being a detective in a mystery story. Upon finding a dead or dying plant, have your child guess what is happening to the plant. Encourage the use of scientific tools and the inquiry process to sup- port or reject guesses.)

- **Use appropriate tools, technology, and techniques to gather, analyze, and interpret data** (For example, encourage the use of the inquiry method in discovering and investigating areas of interest. The steps in the inquiry method are (1) determine what you want to know and what you already know about the subject; (2) get information that already exists about the area of investigation; (3) design a safe investigation to find the answer to the question; (4) conduct the investigation or collect the information or data; (5) organize, analyze, and summarize the findings or information; and (6) redesign the investigation as appropriate to better answer the question.)

- **Organize and maintain a journal showing the procedures and results of an investigation**

- **Develop descriptions, explanations, predictions, and models about the investigation using scientific evidence**

- **Use mathematics when conducting scientific inquiry**

- **Make logical relationships between the evidence and his or her explanations** (For example, together examine a tree stump and count the dark rings to estimate the tree's age. Discuss whether the tree's growth was the same every year, and if not, what could have caused the differences. As your child conducts daily investigations, help him/her make logical connections between the information or data collected and his/her explanations.)

- **Demonstrate effective ways to organize and display scientific data** (For example, have your child use graphic organizers and/or graphs to illustrate findings.)

- **Communicate accurately and clearly about science concepts using scientific words.**

Physical Science - Students apply the principles of motion and forces.

Objective - Students will explore the study of transformations of energy, matter, forces, electricity, and magnetism.

- **Design and complete investigations to calculate the speed (rate of travel) of moving objects** (For example, cut a plastic soda straw to a length of about 4 inches, and thread a string, about 1 yard long, through it. Tie a pencil eraser to each end of the string. Hold the straw upright and move it around in a circular motion so the top weight swings around and around. Change the speed of the rotation, faster and slower, and observe the lower weight. What happens to the lower weight as you increase and decrease the speed of rotation?)

- **Explain the relationship between speed and location of moving objects**
- **Describe how electrical energy is transferred to produce heat, light, sound, and mechanical or chemical energy** (For example, have your child use a flashlight to demonstrate how chemical energy is converted into electrical energy. Suggest that your child share the information with a younger sibling or friend.)

Earth and Space Science - Students learn about the structure of Earth and its position in the solar system.

Objective – Students will continue their study of how air, weather, and climate are related.

- **Demonstrate the relationships of the earth to the sun and the moon**
- **Describe objects that enter the solar system from outside the system** (For example, take a family outing to a local planetarium, or explore comets, meteorites, and micrometeorites on NASA's Web site: **http://kids.msfc.nasa.gov/news/2002/news-mystery.asp/**. The site has great photos, explanations, and activities designed for students.)

Science and Technology - Students learn how science and technology are dependent on each other.

Objective – Students will use technology to create a technological design. They will explore the benefits and consequences of technology within their environment.

- **Identify products or examples of technology that are commonly used**
- **Describe how technology is constantly changing** (For example, computers, medical equipment, and automobiles)
- **Compare the intended benefits and the unintended consequences of technology** (For example, discuss how space technology has been used for tracking icebergs, developing cancer treatments, fighting terrorism and crime, communicating with others around the world, and exploring space. Together, research one example to see if it produced any unintended consequences for humans.)

Science in Personal and Social Perspectives - Students learn to practice safety in science and to evaluate the risks and benefits of science.

Objective – Students will practice safety in science activities; will understand the interrelationships of populations, resources, and environments; and will examine risks and benefits of personal and social decisions.

- **Use precautions when using electrical appliances at home and at school**

- **Describe safety precautions needed during natural hazards** (For example, how to go to a safe room in a house during a tornado, what location in the house is the safest in the event of a natural disaster, and what one should do in the event of an earthquake.)
- **Describe and investigate how student actions impact on world environmental concerns** (For example, help your child identify an environmental cause and research a way he/she can effect change. One example is the Living Planet Pledge from the World Wildlife Federation, available at that organization's Web site: http://www.worldwildlife.org/default.cfm?sectionid=201&newspaperid=11.)

History and Nature of Science - Students understand that science is a human endeavor, understand the cooperation between scientists, and describe events in the history of science.

Objective - Students will explore the history of science and how scientists through time have used new evidence to make changes to theories and accepted ideas.

- **Identify the contributions of individuals from other cultures to knowledge in science, technology, and engineering** (For example, read about a scientist's life and contributions on the Web site Today in Science: http://todayinsci.tripod.com/. Each day the site features scientists who were born on that day of the year.)
- **Recognize and identify types of educational choices required for science and technology careers**
- **Describe how scientists who worked in teams solved a problem or made a scientific discovery** (For example, together watch a movie such as Apollo 16 and discuss how the team worked together on their mission.)
- **Describe and name scientists whose discoveries were ahead of their day.** (For example, read about the life of Jules Verne - a helpful Web site is http://vesuvius.jsc.nasa.gov/er/ seh/bioverne.htm - to learn how, through his studies and writings, he predicted inventions long before they were developed. Together, read one of his books, such as Twenty Thousand Leagues Under the Sea which describes a submarine long before the first plan for a submarine had been drawn.)

Chapter 19

Follow-up

After the production, have the students draw or write about their favorite part of the show. Many disciplines can be used to accomplish this task (e.g., drawing, painting, writing about the presentation, computer aided drawing, word processing).

Below are some of the feedback comments and drawings I received after presenting two shows to an elementary school in London, England.

The teachers wanted to give me a gift for presenting shows for their entire student body, but I told them the greatest gift for me would be for the students to tell me what they liked about the show, what they felt could be improved or what they would like to see in another show.

The teachers had all of the students create one page of their favorite part of the show and bound the pages into a very special book for me to treasure. Here are some of the creative ways students reflected their thoughts on the presentation.

Jan 30, 2004

Dear Mrs. Hart,

Thank you for picking me to be the alien. I like the part when you made the can explode.

Sincerely,
Cody Lokun

The can befor

The can After

Cody Lokun

January
27, 2003

Dear Mrs. Hart,

I like how you showed us magic tricks and I liked the aliens a lot. I also liked when you picked some kids and teachers. And my favorite part was when I got to go in the space ship because it felt like it was real. I liked the show!!

Your friend,
Kai Stridiron

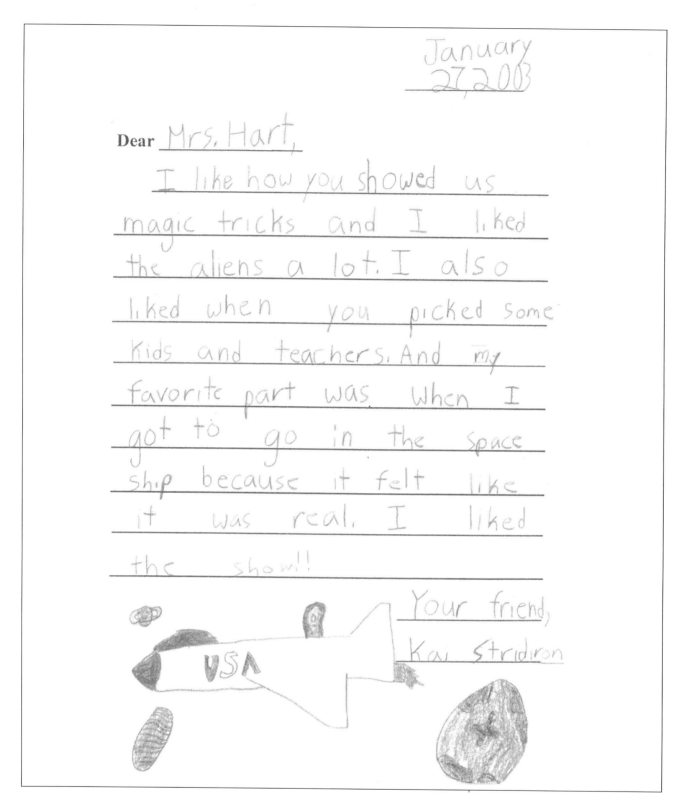

Kai Stridiron

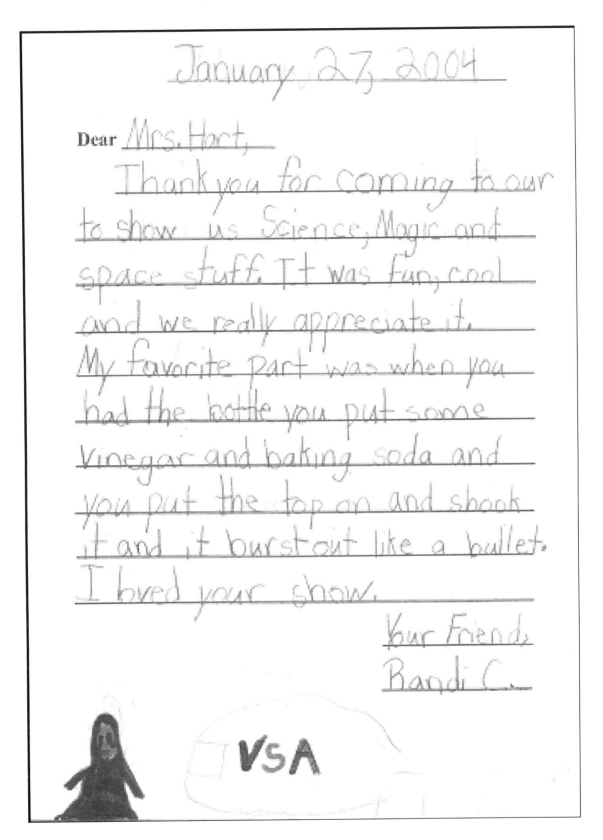

January 27, 2004

Dear Mrs. Hart,

Thank you for coming to our to show us Science, Magic and space stuff. It was fun, cool and we really appreciate it. My favorite part was when you had the bottle you put some vinegar and baking soda and you put the top on and shook it and it burst out like a bullet. I loved your show.

Your Friend,
Randi C.

Randi C.

Callie Steffenhagen (both pictures)

Chloe Rodriguez

Feb. 3, 2004

Dear Mrs. Hart,

I really liked your show. My favorite parts were when the can imploded, because anything imploding is cool. My other favorite part was when you burnt the paper and it just disappeared; now that was just awesome.

It was really nice of you to come and show us your show. The spaceship was pretty neat, even though it wasn't what I thought it would be, but to tell you the truth what it was, was a lot better than what I thought it would be.

Thank you very, very much

Anonymous

Dear Mrs. Hart,

Thank you very much for coming to our school to show us all of your experiments. They were very cool!! My favorite part of your presentation was the part with the burning tissue that disappeared.

Sincerely,
Meghan Byrnes

Meghan Byrnes

Dear Mrs. Hart,

I would like to thank you for the really awesome assembly. I thought the whole assembly was really great. I really liked the part where you made the can implode. The aliens were really funny. That was one of the most amazing assemblies I have ever seen. I think you should make a TV show with your talent. Well I gotta run. See ya.

Anonymous

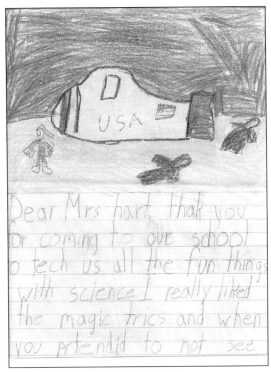

Dear Mrs hart, thak you
or coming to our school
o tech us all the fun things
with science. I really liked
the magic trics. and when
you prtendid to not see

Anonymous

Dear Mrs. Hart,
    Thank you for bringing us the space
show. My favorite was when you heated
the soda can, then dipped it in cold water,
and the can crunched up!!!!

Anonymous

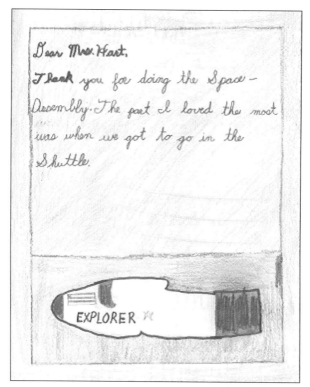

Dear Mrs. Hart,

Thank you for doing the Space-Assembly. The part I loved the most was when we got to go in the Shuttle.

EXPLORER

Anonymous

Dear Mrs. Hart,

Thank you for coming to our school on Math Science Day. I really think that the show you presented was beyond fantastic. Everyone loved the part when you made the can make a pop sound. You showed things we would not try to do. Like when you made the cups with the string and sponge. I thought you just thought that you were going to see if you light the sponge on fire and find out if the string will catch fire. But instead we just made evil laughing sounds with them.

My favorite part of the show was when you lit the handkerchief on fire but nothing had happen to it. To me that was just so great to understand how something can catch fire without getting burned. The show was lovely and I just wanted to say thank you for the show.

Anonymous

Anonymous

Anonymous

Sarah Payne

The end...see you in space.

Chapter 20

Acknowledgements

1. Magic Tricks

http://www.magictricks.com/closeup/invsreel.htm

http://www.hobbytron.net/D'Lite-Soft-Tip-Pair.html?AID=10289758
&PID=1014613

http://www.daytonamagic.com/Fire%20Magic/F01.htm

http://www.magical-tricks.com/FireMagic2.htm

http://www.schoolmasters.com/search.html

http://www.sciencekit.com

http://www.discian.com/resources/tools/hoberman_home.htm

2. The Kevin Eikenberry Group - Hoberman Spheres
http://KevinEikenberry.com

http://www.hobermansphere.com

http://www.school-tech.com/physsci.html

3. Mission Communicators
http://www.farmgoodsforkids.com/um-5005.html

4. Jeff Lindsay's Magic Page
http://www.jefflindsay.com/magic.html#myshow

5. Space Shuttle, Endeavor Script, Shuttle Experiments
The original directions for the larger shuttle given to me at a Science Teacher's Conference in North Carolina in 1996 were written by Renee Coward and Marianna Kesgen and adapted from Dr. Myra Halpin's book, The Enterprise and Beyond. Thank you so much, Dr. Halpin, for letting me use your space shuttle plans in this book. It has been my pleasure talking to you via email and learning how much you love to teach science.

6. Space Shuttle and T-Shirts

U.S. Space Camp (**www.spacecamp.com**) Thank you so much letting me use your logos for the patches, and thank you for permission to use the complete shuttle directions in this book. A special thank you to Mr. Sam Boyd, Ms. Amy Dawkins and the Education Department. I appreciate all of your time and effort into my endeavor.

7. Shuttle Activities

Challenger Center for Space Science Education
www.challenger.org

8. Alien Costumes

http://www.halloweenstreet.com/prod details/id-1703-action-detail

http://www.kidders.com/alien-costume.htm

9. Astronaut Display

http://www.sciplus.com/

http://www.envirosafetyproducts.com/html/disposable coveralls. htm

http://www.safetyinfo.com/equipment/nextgen.htm

http://www.toolprice.com/category/coveralls/

http://www.uvprocess.com/products/Safety/Bodypro/DISPOSABLE COVERALLS.asp

http://www.nitro-pak.com/product info.php/cPath/79 111/ products id/855?os Csid=7dde 1894bd9420a2ef3c30ac51d441ca

10. Curriculum Standards

The Department of Defense Education Activity
http://www.dodea.edu/curriculum/

11. Music

"Mission Control" – Words and Music by Carmino Ravosa from the book World of Music, Silver Burdett & Ginn, 1991. Thank you so much, Mr. Ravosa for letting me use your song "Mission Control" in this book. It has been my pleasure talking to you and especially getting to know you and your wonderful music.

"Mission Control" Words – **http://www.edu-cyberpg.com/ Music/ spacetravel.html**

"Star Wars" Sound Track   "I've Got the Power" by Snap

Appendix A

for

Chapter 3 - Program

Outside and Inside Cover

Space,
Science &
Other Things

Name of School
Principal: Name
Assistant Principal: Name
Your Name: Grade   Room

Date   Time

Picture of your class

Special Thank you

Principal...................................Name

Assistant Principal.................Name

Parents & Volunteers.............Names

Any one else you want to thank.

Program

* Introduction..."Landing of the Endeavor"...all students
* Science is Magic...magic tricks
* "I've Got the Power"...4 audience dancers
* Knowledge is Power...ping pong balls...student names
* Chemical/Physical Changes...magic paper
* Mission: To get students excited about Science and the Science Fair
* Surprise Visitors...student names

SIMPLE SCIENCE EXPERIMENTS

* Matter...Balloons
* Balloon pop with pin...1 audience helper
* Acids/Bases...vinegar & baking soda gases
   • Volcano in a glass
   • Blow balloon up with baking soda/vinegar
   • Blow cork off bottle with baking soda/vinegar
+ Surprise Visitors
* Air Bags...Air Pressure...12 audience helpers
* Sound Vibrations...Chicken Cups...12 audience helpers
* Shuttle Telephone...2 audience helpers
* Surprise Visitors
* Forces:
   • Centrifugal Force...bucket of water
   • Bottle Fountain...1 audience helper
   • Rocket Launcher...2 audience helpers
   • Balloon Race...2 audience helpers
   • Crushing Egg in Hand...12 audience helpers
* Hoberman Sphere – Expanding & Contracting...3 audience helpers

* Crushing Cans with Air Pressure...teacher
* Fire – Handkerchief Experiment...teacher
* Van de Graaf Generator...static electricity, hair raising

FINALE – MISSION CONTROL

CAST
CAPCOM...........STUDENT NAME
FLIGHT DIRECTOR...........STUDENT NAME
MEDICAL OFFICER...........STUDENT NAME
WEATHER PLANE...........STUDENT NAME
COMMANDER...........STUDENT NAME
NAVIGATION...........STUDENT NAME
LAB #1...........STUDENT NAME
PAO #1...........STUDENT NAME
PAO#2...........STUDENT NAME
PILOT...........STUDENT NAME
CREW #1...........STUDENT NAME
CREW #2...........STUDENT NAME
CREW #3...........STUDENT NAME
CREW #4...........STUDENT NAME
CREW #5...........STUDENT NAME
CREW #6...........STUDENT NAME
CREW #7...........STUDENT NAME
DIRECTOR/TEACHER...........YOUR NAME

Thank you for coming to our performance. See you in space!

"Over and out!"

205

Appendix B

for

Chapter 7 – Space Camp
T-Shirts

Names for the back of the T-Shirts

(Copy, cut out and tape on back of shirts)

Goo Goo

ME TOO

CAPCOM

FLIGHT DIRECTOR MEDICAL

OFFICER

WEATHER

PLANE

COMMANDER

NAVIGATION

LAB #1

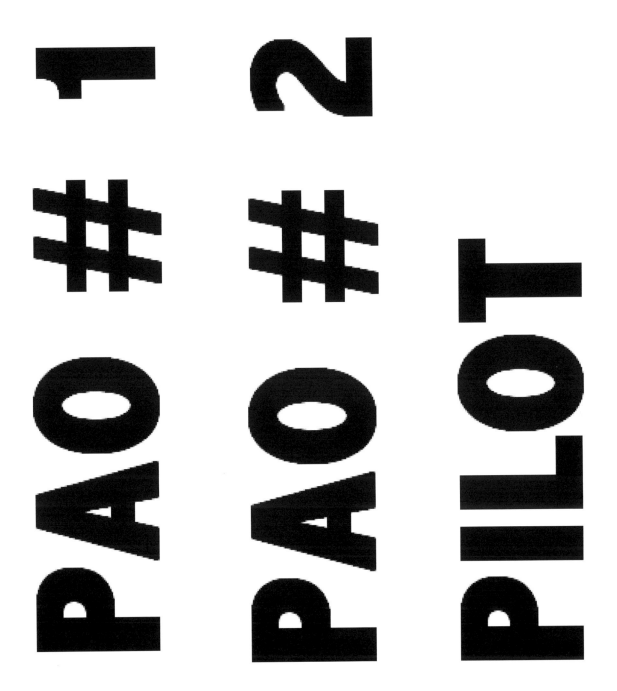

PAO #1

PAO #2

PILOT

MISSION CONTROL CREW #1

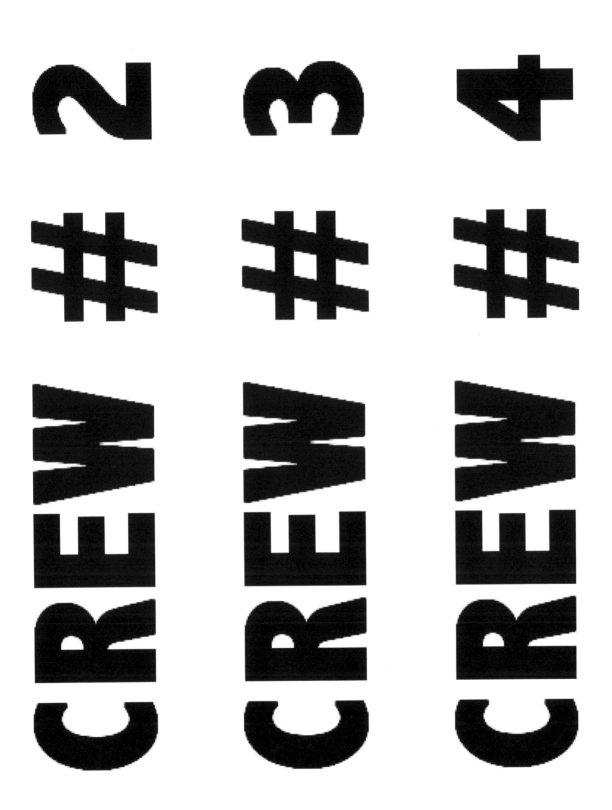

CREW # 5

CREW # 6

CREW # 7

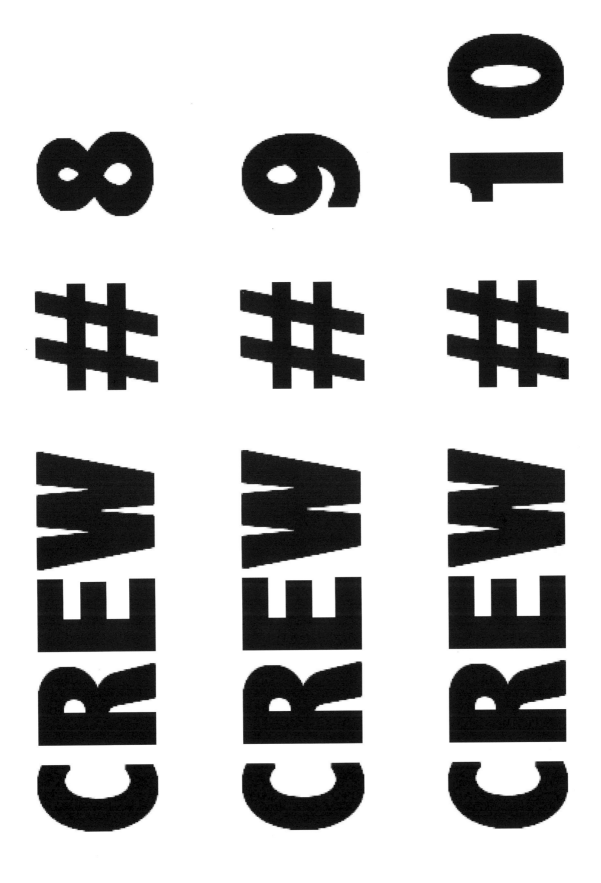

CREW #11

CREW #12

CREW #13

CREW #14

CREW #15

Appendix C

for

Chapter 16
Letters, Permission
Forms, Certificates

Certificates for End of Performance

(Ideas for making certificates)

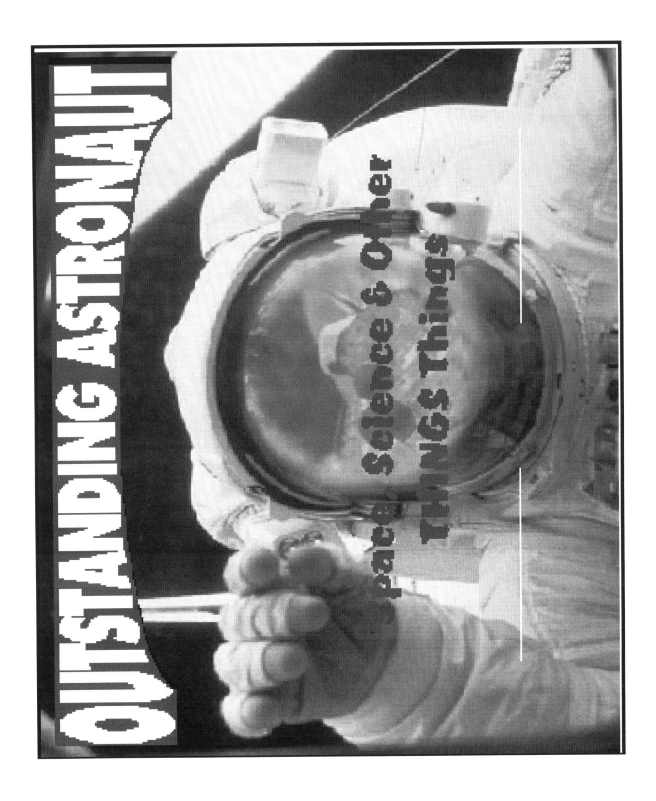

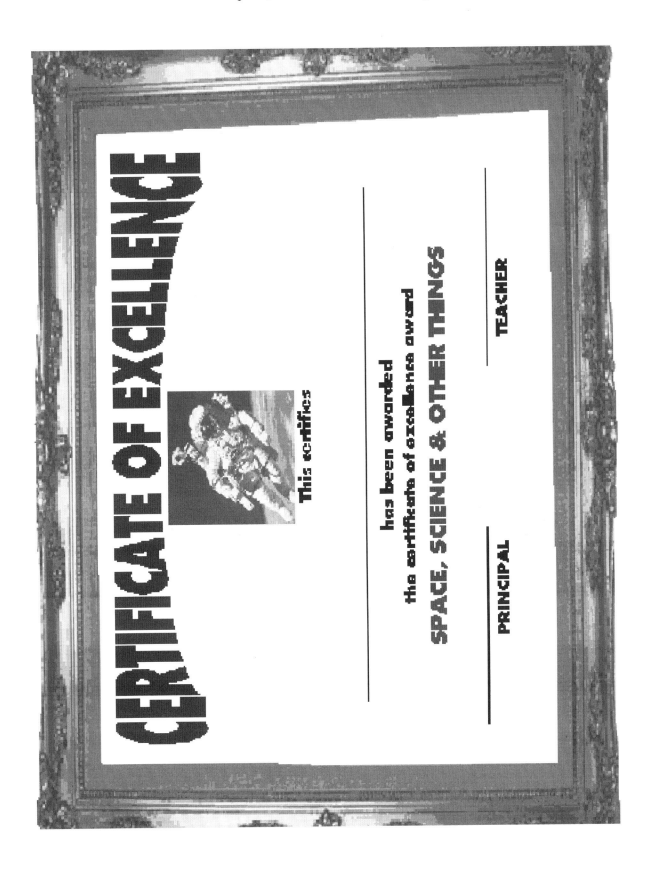

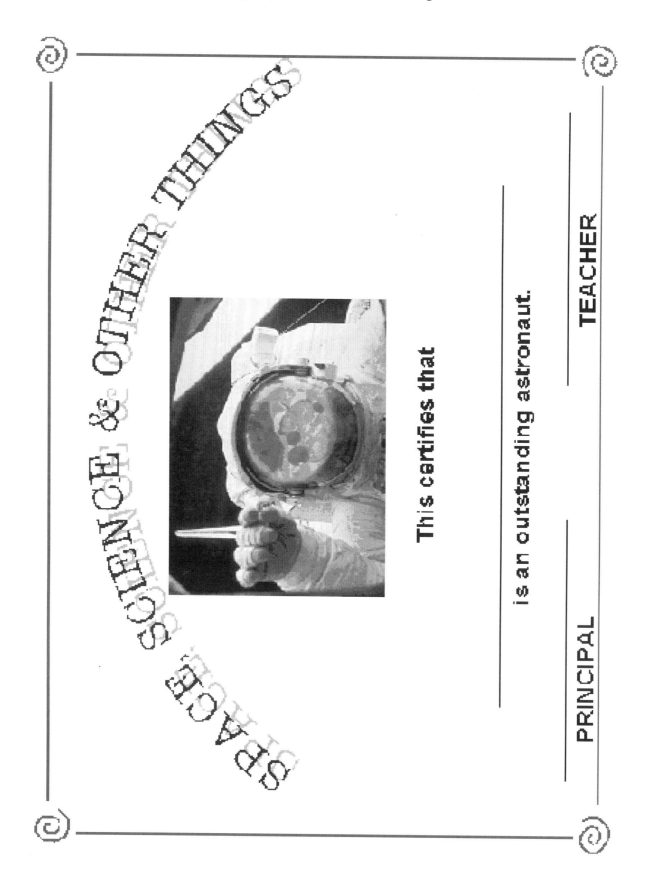

SPACE SCIENCE & OTHER THINGS

This certifies that

is an outstanding astronaut.

PRINCIPAL

TEACHER

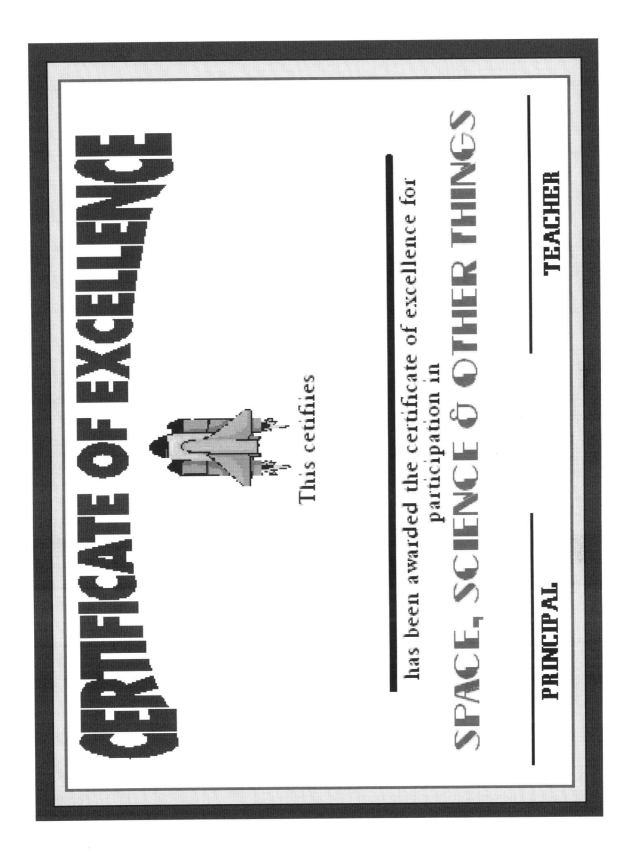

CERTIFICATE OF EXCELLENCE

This certifies

has been awarded the certificate of excellence for
participation in

SPACE, SCIENCE & OTHER THINGS

PRINCIPAL

TEACHER

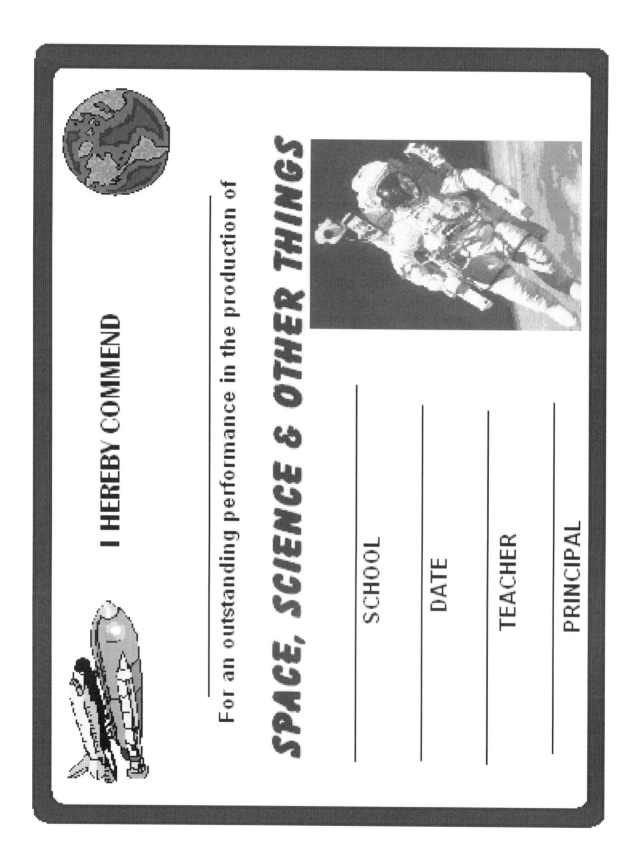

I HEREBY COMMEND

For an outstanding performance in the production of

SPACE, SCIENCE & OTHER THINGS

SCHOOL

DATE

TEACHER

PRINCIPAL

I HEREBY COMMEND

For an outstanding performance in the production of

SPACE, SCIENCE & OTHER THINGS

SCHOOL

DATE

TEACHER

PRINCIPAL

Appendix D

for

Chapter 5

Building the Space Shuttle Orbiter

U.S. Space Camp's Directions

With permission from the Education Department of U.S. Space Camp, Huntsville, AL

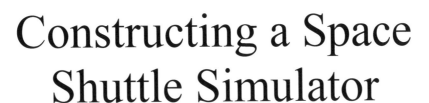

Constructing a Space Shuttle Simulator

Build a Space Shuttle, U.S. Space Camp

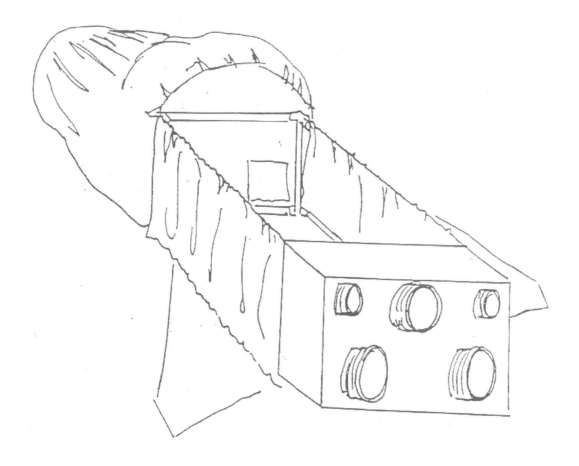

Written by Renée Coward and Marianna Kesgen
Adapted from Myra Halpin's "The Enterprise and Beyond"
Further alterations and additions by the U.S. Space Camp Education Staff

Introduction

I like to think of Space Camp as the world's most inspiring classroom. Here we train aspiring astronauts in the most realistic simulations we can provide. Those we teach may not even notice that they are learning mathematics, science, history and English skills at the same time.

Those who experience the Space Camp magic are always eager to share it with others. This project gives teachers an opportunity to do that by transforming an ordinary school into a NASA training center in just one week. At the beginning of the week the students build part of a space shuttle, a mission control and a space station module, and at the end they become astronauts and NASA personnel for a scripted mission.

Over time this project becomes truly monumental as each group adds their own special touch. The directions that follow, as daunting as they might seem, are only an outline. Feel free to add and modify. The project has never been the same way twice, but it always works.

Preparation

The key to an easy week is preparation and planning. Consider the following:

• **Where are we going to get supplies?**
The items needed are fairly easy to find. Many schools find sponsors such as a local hardware store or solicit donations from parents. Necessary supplies are listed on the next page.

• **Where are we going to build?**
Usually the shuttle, station and mission control fill half of a standard Elementary school gymnasium. Any indoor space of this size should be acceptable. Consider where each part of the project will fit before committing to a location.

• **Who will supervise?**
Students do all of the building, but it is important to have teachers or parent volunteers around to help each small group of students.

• **How many students will be building at a time?**
Ideally 12-13 students should be building in each 45 minutes to one hour time period. These students are usually given different tasks. For example one group could be working on mission control while the other tapes together the Space Station. Like any part of the project, this can be adapted.

• **What else will the students be doing?**
This project is usually done as part of a Space Week. Teachers often choose to conduct other space related activities with students who are not building.

Typical Week

SUNDAY
Evaluate space, check supplies and discuss logistics.
Set up each workstation.
Construct copy paper box mounts for Mission Control.

MONDAY
Briefly discuss the purposes of the space shuttle.
Begin construction at all stations.

TUESDAY
Briefly discuss how the space shuttle operates.
Continue construction at all stations.

WEDNESDAY
Complete construction.
Conduct a brief mission walk through.

THURSDAY
Conduct missions.

FRIDAY
Conduct missions.

Supply List

Make sure that items that are **donated** and are to be **returned** to people have names written somewhere on the item. Also, it is nice to keep track of who donates supplies (especially the large amounts) so that you may write "Thank You" notes.

Quantity	Description	Approximate Cost
1 roll	Polyethylene film, clear, 6 mil, 100' x 12'	$30/100' roll
12 feet	Laminate film, run through the laminator	School supplies
15 rolls	Clear Packing Tape (Duck Brand)	$3.50 each
2	Box Window Fans	$20.00 ea ($5 @ thrift store
360'	¾" PVC pipe, 480 psi, Schedule 40	$0.20/foot
45	¾" PVC T Joints	$0.30 each
30	¾" PVC L Joints	$0.30 each
2	PVC pipe cutter	$10.00 each
1	Twin flat sheet (2 is even better!)	$3.00

6	White Vinyl Shower Curtain Liner	$2.50 each
6 packages	Shower Curtain Rings	
1 large roll	White Butcher Paper (at least 50 yards)	School Supplies
1 roll	Black Butcher Paper (50 yards)	School Supplies
1	Carpet Roll (empty), or about 24 sheets posterboard	Donation
3	Empty 3- or 5- gallon buckets (restaurants get pickles, kool-aid or chips in them)	Donation
12	Black permanent markers	Donation
12-18	Packs of good (Crayola) markers	
12	Pencils	School supplies
1	Large can of tempera school paint in various colors, esp. red, yellow, black & white	School supplies
6	Yardsticks and/or Measuring Tape	School Supplies
	String	School Supplies
2	Box Cutters with extra blades	Donation
	Scraps of red, orange and yellow tissue/ const. paper	School Supplies
15-20 rolls	Aluminum Foil	Donation
2 rolls	Grey Duct Tape	$3 ea
2 rolls	Black Duct Tape	$3 ea.
2	Masking Tape	$1 ea
2	Electrical Tape	$2 ea.
12	Scissors (sharp, various sizes)	$4 ea.
1	Pictures of Flags of 16 ISS partners	Space Camp CD
2	Refrigerator boxes (with tops and bottoms)	Donation
1	Washing machine box (with top and bottom)	Donation
15	Copy paper boxes	Donation/School
15	Lite-Brites and at least 5 bags of extra pegs	Donation
	Extra cardboard boxes for satellite construction	Donation

PVC Preparation

As others begin the instructions on the next page have several students measure the ¾" PVC pipe to the dimensions listed in the diagram on the next page. After each portion is measured an adult should cut it with the PVC cutters. The students should collect each set of pieces, wrap them with masking tape and label them with the area and length. For example the first set of pieces would be labeled, "Orbiter 5 feet."

Group	Quantity	Length
Orbiter	10	5 feet
	8	3 feet
	8	3 to 3½ inches
Station	10	5 feet
	8	3 feet
	8	3 to 3½ inches
Payload Bay	16	5 feet
	16	3 feet
	10	3 to 3½ inches
Wings	4	9 feet
	2	4 feet
	2	2 feet

Orbiter Crew Cabin (½ scale)

Astronaut Scott Horowitz once said that going to space is just like going camping. Astronauts sleep in sleeping bags and eat camping food. They even do all of this in a place known as the crew cabin. The crew cabin provides a cockpit, living space and a laboratory.

1. Roll out a 25' by 15' rectangle of polyethylene film.

2. Cut an isosceles triangle template out of cardboard with a base of 12" and a height of 7'

3. Use this template to outline 12 triangles on the 25' length of the polyethylene film. Each triangle should be 13" apart.

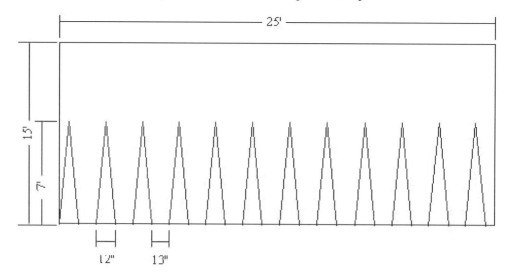

4. Cut out and discard the 12 triangles.

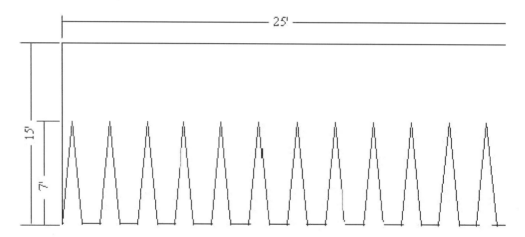

* **Every seam should be reinforced on either side of the original piece of tape. It is important to remind the students to pull the tape slowly and to push it to the plastic no more than half foot at a time. This will prevent the tape from pulling apart when the orbiter or station is inflated.**

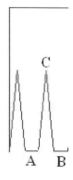

5. Overlapping the edges slightly, tape AC to BC. Repeat until all 12 triangles have been taped together. (For added strength, tape both sides of any cut edges.)

6. Tape DE to FG. This will create a cylinder or "sleeve" with ends open.

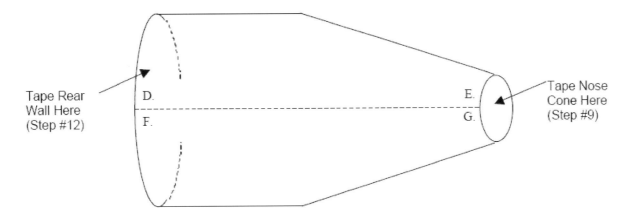

Tape Rear
Wall Here
(Step #12)

D.
F.

E.
G.

Tape Nose
Cone Here
(Step #9)

7. Cut out a 4' by 12' rectangle of polyethylene film. This will become the nose cone and the fan sleeve of the orbiter. Cut out the 4' by 4' nose cone square. Set aside the 4' by 8' fan sleeve for later use.

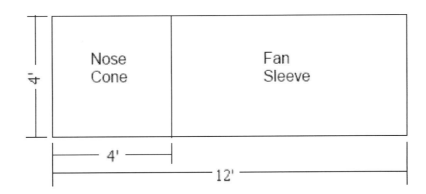

Nose
Cone

Fan
Sleeve

4'

4'

12'

8. Nose Cone: Locate the center of the nose cone square by folding it in quarters. Tie a marker to a two-foot long string. Holding the other end of the string at the center of the square, draw a circle with a radius of two feet. Cut out the circle.

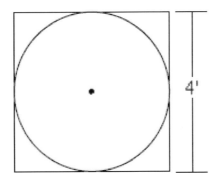

4'

9. Tape the nose cone to the small end of the main cabin body. (This is a little cumbersome—make it fit!)

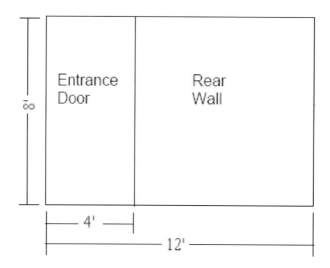

10. Rear Wall: Cut the 8' by 12' polyethylene film into a 4' by 8' rectangle and a 8' by 8' square. Reserve the 4' by 8' piece for the entrance door.

11. Locate the center of the square by folding it into quarters. Tie a marker to a four foot long string. Holding the other end of the string at the center of the square, draw a circle having a radius of four feet. Cut out the circle.

12. Tape the rear wall circle to the large end of the main cabin body.

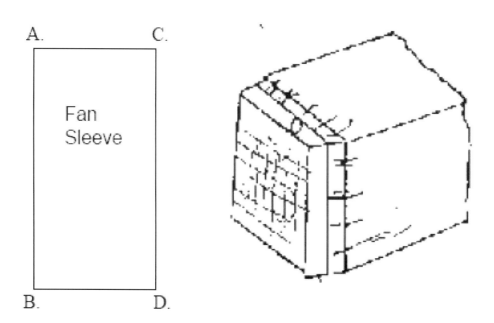

13. Fan Sleeve: Retrieve the 4' by 8' rectangle (step #7). Using the box fan as a guide overlap and tape side AC with side BD so the sleeve fits snuggly around the fan.

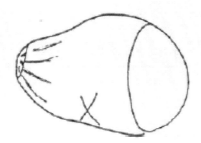 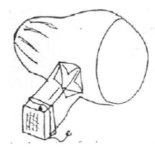

14. Decide where to place the fan that will inflate the orbiter cabin. Think about the location of outlets, which way the orbiter will face and where the space station will be before making a decision. On the side of the orbiter you choose cut an "X" to make an opening about 8 inches from the bottom. It is better to place this too low than too high; the sides of the cabin will lift up after it is inflated.

15. Use the sides of the "X" to join the fan sleeve to the orbiter cabin body. Tape this loosely (It can be secured better after completing the entrance porthole.) Turn the fan on at the highest setting to inflate the orbiter.

16. With the orbiter cabin inflated; cut an entrance out of the rear wall close to the floor. This should be large enough to fit a person, but not large enough to allow much air to escape.

17. Door: Retrieve the 4' by 8' piece of polyethylene film and fold in half to form a 4' square. Tape the open edges together. This will be used to reinforce the door.

18. Floor Mat: Cut two 6' by 6' pieces of polyethylene film. Place one on top of the other and tape the edges to form a two-layer floor mat.

19. Crawl into the orbiter cabin through the opening cut in step 16. When entering the orbiter cabin it is best to remove shoes and crawl very close to floor to prevent the hole from getting larger. Once inside cut a small (approx. 3" - 4") "X" in the ceiling to allow air to circulate through the cabin.

20. From the inside tape the door square over the opening. Tape only the top and half of the left and right sides so that a person can still crawl inside. The air from the fan should push this door flap against the opening to prevent too much air from escaping.

21. Tape the floor mat to the floor.

22. From the inside also secure the seam between the fan sleeve and the cabin. Have others secure it from the outside.

23. Tape and reinforce the inside of all seams from inside the orbiter cabin. Have one person stand outside and push the tape against his or her hand for support.

24. PVC Pipe Framework for the Orbiter Cabin: The PVC pipe framework inside the orbiter cabin is designed to provide a protective casing in case the fan should lose power. It also serves provides a place to suspend a sheet designed to represent the flight deck panel. Retrieve the PVC pieces cut earlier for the orbiter framework and construct the structure as shown below.

25. When complete tape each joint with clear tape except the L-joints at the front top of the structure.

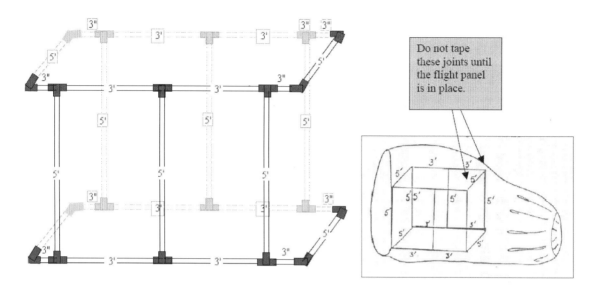

Quantity	Length
10	5 feet
8	3 feet
8	3 to 3½ inches

26. Use lamination film to create windows in the orbiter. Cut a piece of lamination film into four approximately 1' by 1'6" rectangles. Tape these on the front of the orbiter with clear tape as shown in the picture on the right.

27. From the inside of the orbiter remove the polyethylene film from the areas covered by the new windows and tape the seams with clear tape.

28. For decoration cover the outside edge of each window with duct tape. Then tape a line of electrical tape down the center of each piece of duct tape.

29. Draw and paint a school mascot approximately 2' by 2' on a piece of white butcher paper.

30. Cut a 4'diameter circle from a roll of black butcher paper. Attach the school mascot to the circle and tape it to the orbiter's nose cone.

31. On a flat sheet draw a flight panel. This should contain the screens, dials, switches and buttons needed to fly the space shuttle. These can be labeled with anything from "Landing Gear" to "Press for Pizza." Just be certain that the hem of the sheet is on top.

32. Remove the 5' piece from the top front of the Orbiter PVC structure. Cut either end of the sheet hem and slide the PVC through. Replace the PVC and tape it. Now when the students look at the front of the cabin they will see the switches and panels they created.

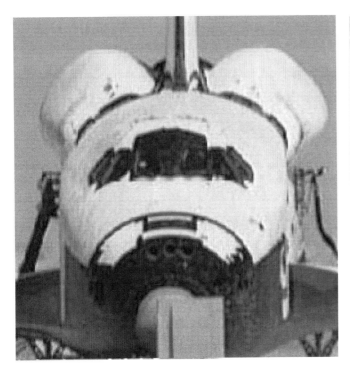

Shuttle Cockpit

Payload Bay

If the crew cabin is the astronaut's home in space, the Payload Bay is their garage. The payload bay of an actual orbiter is large enough to carry a school bus to space, but usually the payload bay is used to carry satellites, pieces of the space station, and supplies for the space station or experiments.

1. Cargo Bay PVC Framework: Construct a rectangular "box" of dimensions 12 foot by 5 foot using the PVC pipes (see diagram).

2. Tape each joint of the structure and use extra PVC to reinforce the structure if necessary.

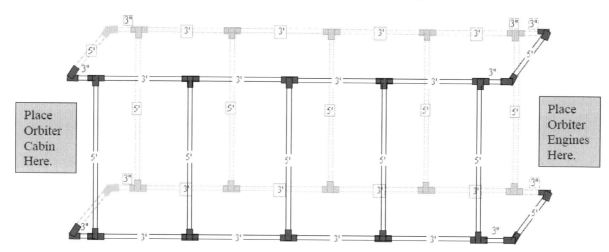

Quantity	Length
16	5 feet
16	3 feet
10	3 to 3½ inches

3. Unfold the six white shower curtains. Use a yardstick and a Sharpie marker to trace the fold lines. These rectangles will represent orbiter heat tiles.

4. Hang the shower curtains from the sides of the PVC structure. Cut off any excess.

5. Place the words, NASA and United States, on the walls and/or display the names of the school or sponsors.

Orbiter Wings

When the orbiter lands it is more of a glider than a plane since its powerful engines are not used during landing. This means that the pilots have only one chance to make a perfect landing, so well made orbiter wings are essential.

1. Retrieve the PVC pipe pieces cut earlier for the Orbiter Wings. There should be two 9-foot pieces, one 4-foot piece and one 2-foot piece for each wing.

2. Use these to construct the quadrilateral shown in the diagram below. Use L-joints to connect two joints and securely tape the others. Repeat this process for the second wing.

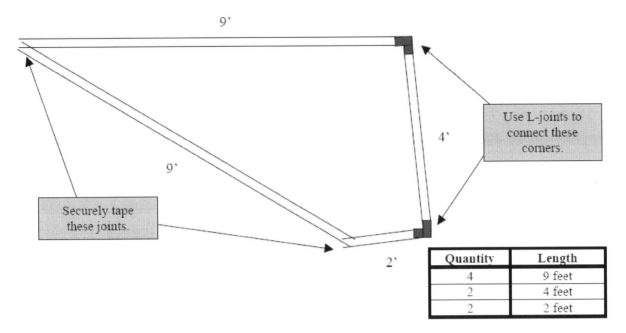

Quantity	Length
4	9 feet
2	4 feet
2	2 feet

3. Turn one wing upside down so that it is the mirror image of the other. Cover both wings with white paper.

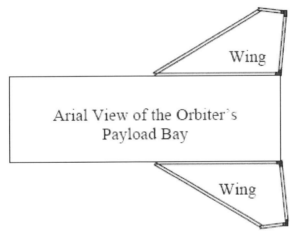

4. If desired place the letters, "USA" on the right wing and an American flag on the left wing.

Orbiter Aft

The word aft refers to the back of portion of the orbiter. This will house the powerful Space Shuttle Main Engines (SSMEs) used during launch and the smaller Orbital Maneuvering System Engines (OMS) used to move in space.

1. Cut 1-foot long pieces from the carpet roll with a saw.
2. Wrap two refrigerator boxes in black butcher paper.
3. Place the two boxes on top of each other.

4. Determine the placement of the three main engines (to be represented by three-gallon buckets) and the two OMS engines (to be represented by the carpet roll sections). Cut an appropriately sized "X" at each location.

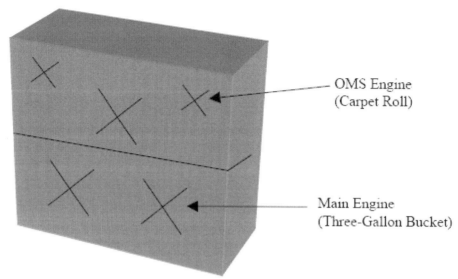

OMS Engine
(Carpet Roll)

Main Engine
(Three-Gallon Bucket)

5. Place the three gallon buckets and the carpet roll sections in the appropriate places. Tear long strips of yellow, orange and red paper and tape it inside each engine to represent flames.

6. If desired create a vertical stabilizer using the picture as a guide.

Vertical

Stablizer

Space Station

When completed the International Space Station will be as long as a football ball and nearly as wide. It would be nearly impossible to launch something so large all at once, so it was divided into smaller pieces. These directions are for a type of piece known as a module. Modules provide working and living space for astronauts. The finished station will have many to house several astronauts for months at a time.

1. Roll out a 25' by 12' rectangle of polyethylene film

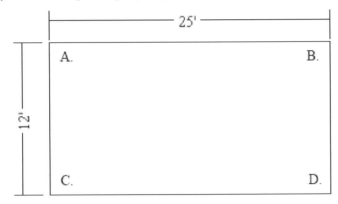

2. Tape AB to CD to create a cylinder with two open ends.

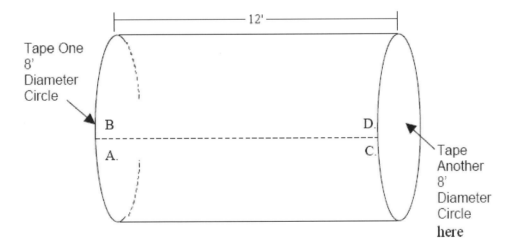

3. Cut out two 8' by 8' squares of polyethylene film.

4. Locate the center of one of these squares by folding it in quarters. Tie a marker to a four-foot long string. Hold the end of the string on this point and draw a circle with a radius of four feet. Cut out the circle. Repeat the process with the second square. Tape these to the ends of the space station to close the cylinder.

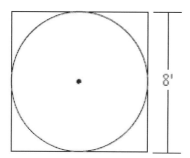

5. Fan Sleeve: Cut a 4' by 8' rectangle. Using the box fan as a guide overlap and tape side AC with side BD so that the sleeve fits snuggly around the fan.

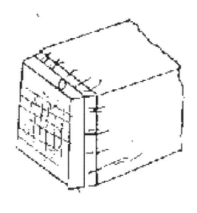

6. On the side farthest away from the space station cut an "X" to make an opening about 8 inches from the bottom. It is better to place this too low than too high; the sides of the station module will lift up after it is inflated.

7. Use the sides of the "X" to join the fan sleeve to the station body. Tape this loosely (It can be secured better after completing the entrance porthole.) Turn the fan on at the highest setting to inflate the station.

8. With the station module inflated; cut an entrance out of the rear wall close to the floor. This should be large enough to fit a person, but not large enough to allow much air to escape.

9. Door: Cut a 4' by 8' piece of polyethylene film and fold in half to form a 4' square. Tape the open edges together. This will be used to reinforce the door.

10. Floor Mat: Cut two 6' by 6' pieces of polyethylene film. Place one on top of the other and tape the edges to form a two-layer floor mat.

11. Crawl into the station through the opening cut in step 16. When entering the orbiter cabin it is best to remove shoes and crawl very close to floor to prevent the hole from getting larger. Once inside cut a small (approx. 3" - 4") "X" in the ceiling to allow air to circulate.

12. From the inside tape the door square over the opening. Tape only the top and half of the left and right sides so that a person can still crawl inside. The air from the fan should push this door flap against the opening to prevent too much air from escaping.

13. Tape the floor mat to the floor.

14. From the inside also secure the seam between the fan sleeve and the cabin. Have others secure it from the outside.

15. Tape and reinforce the inside of all seams from inside the orbiter cabin. Have one person stand outside and push the tape against his or her hand for support.

16. PVC Pipe Framework: The PVC pipe framework inside the station is designed to provide a protective casing in case the fan should lose power. It also serves provides a place to suspend a sheet designed to represent the flight deck panel. Retrieve the PVC pieces cut earlier for the station framework and construct the structure as shown below.

17. When complete tape each joint with clear tape.

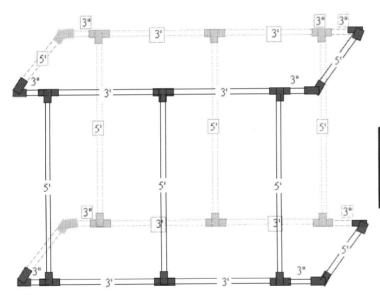

Quantity	Length
10	5 feet
8	3 feet
8	3 to 3½ inches

18. Use lamination film to create a large window in the station. Generally this is in the front of the station so that the audience can see inside. Cut a piece of lamination film to the desired size. Tape this on the station with clear tape.

19. From the inside of the station remove the polyethylene film from the areas covered by the new windows and tape the seams with clear tape.

20. For decoration cover the outside edge of each window with duct tape. Then tape a line of electrical tape down the center of each piece of duct tape.

21. If you have another twin sheet, have the students design experiment and galley racks. This should contain the screens, dials, switches and buttons needed to live in space for long periods of time. These can be labeled with anything from "Ant Farm Experiment" to "Emergency Food Supply." Just be certain that the hem of the sheet is on top.

22. Create a sign that says, "International Space Station." Tape this on the exterior of the station.

23. Create one flag for each country involved with the International Space Station (see below). All flags should be about 24" x 14". Tape the finished flags to the exterior of the Space Station. If desired label each of the flags.

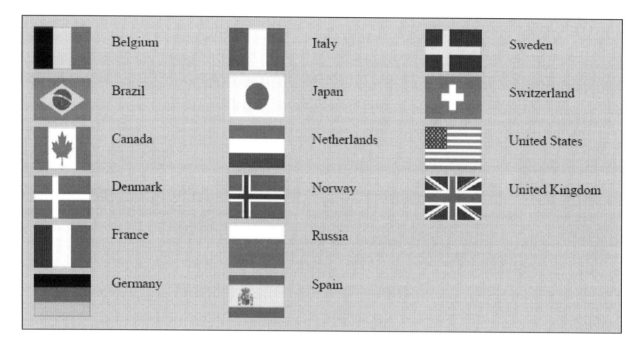

24. Create solar panels by wrapping two rectangular scraps of cardboard with aluminum foil and duct tape. Tape these to the floor outside the station.

Tunnel

The tunnel connects the orbiter and space station so the students can crawl from one to the other during the mission. It is important that the tunnel is large enough to fit the kids, but not so large that the station and orbiter begin to deflate.

1. Push the space station and orbiter so that they are no more than four feet apart.

2. Cut a 5' by 7' piece of polyethylene film.

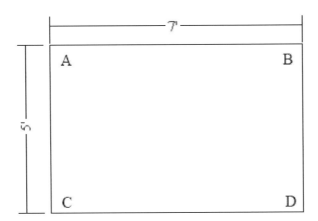

3. Tape AC to BD to form a cylinder. Reinforce the seam, turn the cylinder inside out and tape the inside seam.

4. Loosely tape the tunnel so that it connects the orbiter and the space station.

5. From the inside of each, cut an "X" in walls of the orbiter and the space station where the tunnel connects.

6. Tape the tunnel from the inside and outside with copious amounts of tape until it is secure.

Mission Control

It takes hundreds of people to make a shuttle launch happen. In any mission dozens of the most brilliant people in NASA are gathered together to command the mission and to solve any problems that might arise. Their computers keep track of the orbiter, the space station and the astronauts.

Complete the following steps before the students arrive to work:

1. Obtain 12 to 16 copy paper boxes. Remove the lids from the boxes.

2. On the back of each box trace a Lite Bright. Cut the lines out with a box cutter.

3. Wrap each of the boxes with white butcher paper.

4. Cut an "X" on the side with the Lite Bright sized holes.

5. On the opposite side cut a small hole and push the cord through from the inside.

6. Insert the Lite Bright. It should fit snuggly. Secure it with tape.

7. Place the blank Lite Bright papers into each Lite Bright. Secure these with tape.

8. Retrieve the half of the box lids. Each lid will be used to make two keyboards.

9. Cut each lid in half lengthwise. Wrap these in White Butcher paper.

10. Find a suitable location for Mission Control. Find multiple tables. Cover the tops with white butcher paper.

11. Tape the monitors and keyboards to the top of the tables.

12. Use power strips and extension cords to plug in each Lite Bright.

Have the students complete the remaining steps throughout the week:

1. Create name placards for each position in Mission Control (15 total). Fold an 8½" x 11" piece of paper in half "hot dog" style. On one side write the positions listed below and add decorations. Tape the completed signs on the top of each mission control consul.

PAO (Public Affairs Officer)	Booster Engineer
PAYCOM (Payloads Communicator)	Ground Controller
Flight Director	INCO (Integrated Communication Officer)
CAPCOM (Capsule Communicator)	RIO (Russian Interface Officer)
PROP (Propulsions Engineer)	DPS (Data Processing System Engineer)
Flight Surgeon	Launch/Landing Director
FIDO (Flight Dynamics Officer)	Weather
Guidance	

2. Decorate each Lite Bright with colored pegs. The students can copy world or U.S. maps, write a countdown ("10, 9, 8 . . .") or recreate weather reports and pictures of the shuttle. Creativity is key.

3. Draw keys on each of the cardboard keyboards using an actual computer keyboard as a guide.

4. On butcher paper draw a large map to mount in mission control. Create other decorations as needed.

Satellite

The orbiter has deployed and repaired many satellites. Some of these look down to learn about the Earth and others look to the heavens to learn about the universe. Others make cell phones and satellite television a reality. The trainees will be building an MTV satellite * *following the rough guidelines below.*

1. Find a box or several boxes to form the body of the satellite.

2. Wrap the boxes in Aluminum Foil.

3. Cut holes and insert a scrap piece of PVC pipe through the center of the satellite.

4. Cut rectangular scrap pieces of cardboard to form solar panels. Wrap these in aluminum foil and tape them to the PVC pipe.

5. Decorate the satellite and place it near the Payload Bay.

Create an experiment rack for the space station. This can be constructed from a box wrapped with white butcher paper. Its dimensions should not exceed 1½' x 1½' x 4'.

Final Preparations

Now the space shuttle is nearly ready for launch. Complete the following steps before mission day to be completely ready.

• Scripts
Make certain the students are practicing their scripts well before the mission. Each student should have a part. If there are more parts than students assign two consecutively numbered mission control parts to one student (e.g., Mission Control 1 and Mission Control 2). On the day before the mission conduct a walk through. Have the students take their places and tell them how to move throughout the mission.

• Sound System
It is important that the students in all areas of the mission can hear each other. If possible place 2-4 microphones in Mission Control, one in the orbiter, one in the space station, and have a cordless microphone available for the spacewalks.

• Tape Scripts
No one wants to take a script with them on their spacewalk. Find the pages for both spacewalks. Highlight the mission specialist parts and tape them to the side of the satellite and next to the station solar panels where they can be seen.

• Seats for Audience
Find a place out of the way to seat any visitors.

• Experiments to Space Station
A space station wouldn't be a space station without experiments. Place a hydroponic garden or other experiments inside the station module and have a report available for the students to read.